Corsica
Travel Guide

The Ultimate Travel Guide to Exploring the Hidden Gems Of Corsica

Greene Peterson

ALL RIGHTS RESERVED. NO PART OF THIS PUBLICATION MAY BE REPRODUCED, DISTRIBUTED, OR TRANSMITTED IN ANY FORM OR BY ANY MEANS, INCLUDING PHOTOCOPYING, RECORDING, OR OTHER ELECTRONIC OR MECHANICAL METHODS, WITHOUT THE PRIOR WRITTEN PERMISSION OF THE PUBLISHER, EXCEPT IN THE CASE OF BRIEF QUOTATIONS EMBODIED IN CRITICAL REVIEWS AND CERTAIN OTHER NONCOMMERCIAL USES PERMITTED BY COPYRIGHT LAW.

COPYRIGHT © GREENE PETERSON

Table of Contents

Brief History 8
Geography 11
Tourists Must Know Things Before Visiting 14
Top Activities 17
    Hiking 17
    Beach hopping 20
    Scuba diving 23
    Canyoning 26
    Rock climbing 29
    River rafting 31
    Horseback riding 34
    Mountain biking 37
    Sea kayaking 40
    Paragliding 43
Dialects and Language 46
Weather 48
Getting Here 50
Top Attractions 53
    Calvi Citadel 53
    Bonifacio 56
    Scandola Nature Reserve 59
    Corte 62

Porto-Vecchio 65
Aiguilles de Bavella 68
Palombaggia Beach 70
Filitosa 72
Piana Calanches 74
L'Île-Rousse 77
Propriano 80
Genoese Tower 83
Monte d'Oro 86
Museums and Cultural Sites 89
Corsican Vineyards 91

Top Cuisine to Try Out 94
Fiadone 94
Civet de Sanglier.. 97
Brocciu 99
Figatellu 101
Salsiccia 103
Aubergine à la Bonifacienne 105
Soupe Corse 107
Grilled Seafood 109
Falculelle 111
Cannelloni 113
Patrimonio Wine 115

4

Best Time To Visit 117
Traveling Itinerary 120
    1 Week Itinerary for Corsica 120
    2 Week Itinerary for Corsica 121
Visiting On a Budget 124
Getting Around 127
Shopping for Souvenirs 131
Tour Package Options 135
Tourist Safety Tips 139
Festival and Events 142

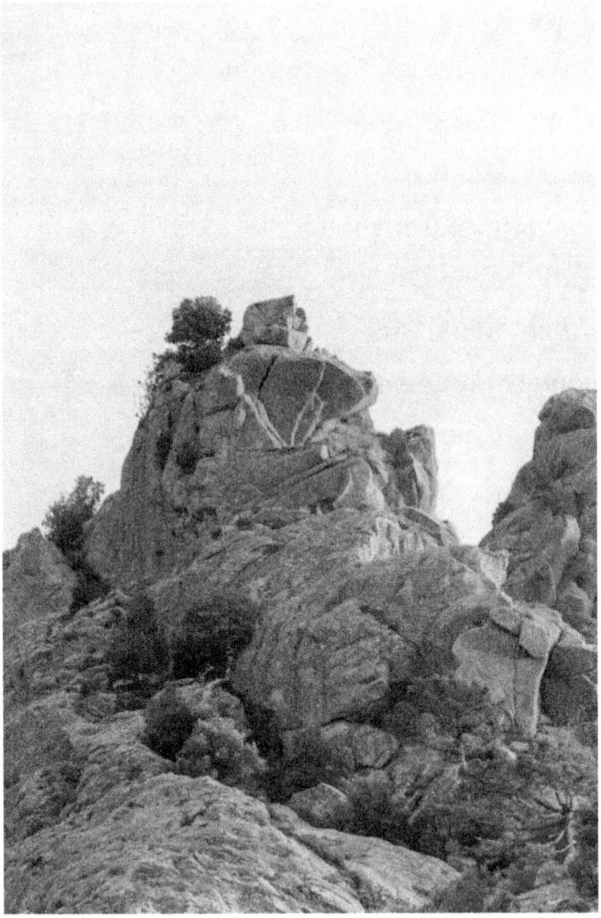

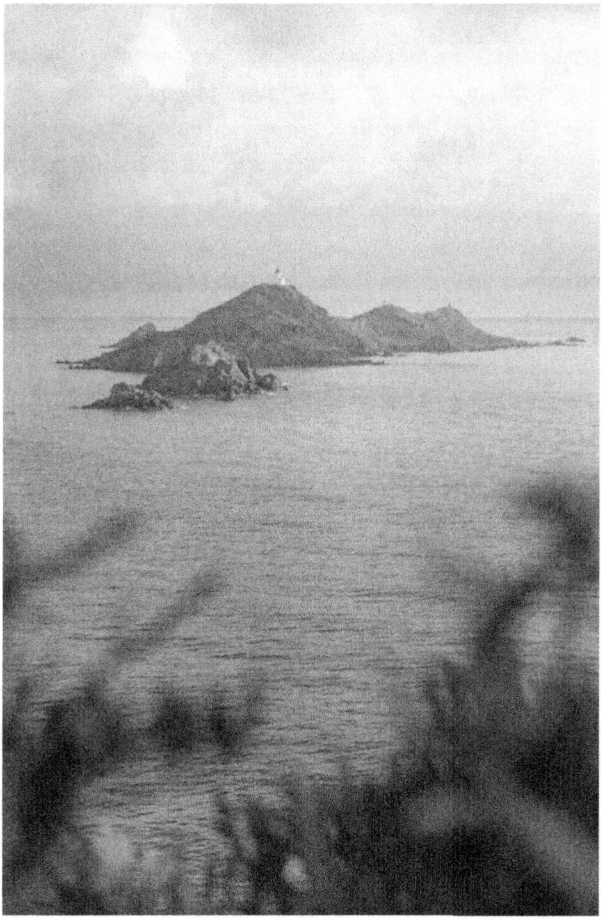

Brief History

Corsica, an island located in the Mediterranean Sea, has a rich and stormy history that spans thousands of years. From ancient settlements to Roman conquests, through medieval wars to modern efforts for autonomy, the history of Corsica is rich with remarkable events and cultural influences.

Corsica's history begins in prehistoric periods, with evidence of human occupancy on the island dating back to the Mesolithic period approximately 10,000 BCE. The island was then inhabited by different tribes, including the Etruscans and Ligurians, before being captured by the ancient Greeks in the 6th century BCE. Corsica was thereafter dominated by the Romans, who created colonies and built highways and cities, leaving a lasting imprint on the island's culture and architecture.

During the Middle Ages, Corsica witnessed multiple invasions and changes in rulership. It was taken by the Vandals in the 5th century, followed by the Byzantines in the 6th century. In the 9th century, Corsica was invaded by the Moors from North Africa, who established a brief dominion until being pushed out by native Corsican nobility.

In the 11th century, Corsica came under the sovereignty of the Republic of Pisa, a coastal city-state in Italy. However, Pisa's power was challenged by other Italian city-states, such as Genoa, which progressively gained control of Corsica in the 13th century. Genoa's sovereignty over Corsica was often disputed, and the island experienced repeated wars and skirmishes as several local lords and aristocratic families vied for supremacy.

In the late 18th century, Corsica came under the influence of the French, who seized the island in 1769 after crushing the Corsican resistance led by Pasquale Paoli. Corsica was then included in the French realm and later became a French province. During this time, Corsica witnessed substantial cultural and societal changes, as French laws, language, and administration were imposed on the island.

Corsica's history is also marked by its struggle for independence and autonomy. Throughout the 19th and 20th centuries, there were various upheavals and movements for Corsican nationalism, with demands for more autonomy and acknowledgment of Corsican identity. Some famous characters in Corsican histories, like as Pasquale Paoli and Napoleon Bonaparte, were noted for their participation in championing Corsican independence.

In recent years, Corsica has been granted a degree of autonomy within France, with a regional government and limited powers of self-governance. However, the issue of Corsican autonomy and independence remains a difficult topic, with constant debates and discussions between Corsican nationalists and the French government.

Corsica's history is also reflected in its unique cultural heritage. Corsican culture is a combination of numerous influences, including Italian, French, and Mediterranean traditions. The Corsican language, known as Corsu or Corsican, is a Romance language closely linked to Italian, but with its specific dialects and peculiarities. Corsican cuisine is also known for traditional dishes incorporating local ingredients, such as chestnuts, cheeses, and cured meats.

From ancient settlements to Roman authority, from medieval wars to modern aspirations for independence, Corsica's history has molded its unique culture and identity. Today, Corsica remains a fascinating tourist destination, offering visitors a glimpse into its rich and diverse history.

Geography

Corsica is one of the 18 regions of France and has a unique geography that sets it apart from other islands in the region.

Corsica is located roughly 170 kilometers (105 miles) west of Italy, 80 kilometers (50 miles) southeast of the French mainland, and 12 kilometers (7.5 miles) north of the island of Sardinia, Italy. It has a total area of around 8,680 square kilometers (3,350 square miles), making it the fourth-largest island in the Mediterranean.

The environment of Corsica is defined by its rocky and mountainous terrain. The island is dominated by a mountain range known as the Corsican Mountains, which are part of the broader Ligurian Alps. Mount Cinto is the tallest mountain on the island, reaching an elevation of 2,706 meters (8,878 feet). The Corsican Mountains are noted for their majestic peaks, deep valleys, and gorgeous rivers, which form a breathtaking environment.

Corsica's coastline is about 1,000 kilometers (620 miles) long, with various coves, capes, and sandy beaches. The island is also home to several natural harbors, notably the Gulf of Porto and the Gulf of Ajaccio. Corsica's coastline is noted for its picturesque beauty and is a popular location for tourists, with many visitors enjoying activities like as swimming, snorkeling, and boating.

The island has a Mediterranean climate, with hot, dry summers and warm, wet winters. The climate is affected by the Mediterranean Sea and the Corsican Mountains, which generate microclimates around the island. Corsica has considerable rainfall throughout the winter months, which feeds its rivers and provides rich flora, including forests of oak, chestnut, and pine trees. In contrast, the summer months are hot and dry, with low rainfall, which contributes to the island's Mediterranean climate.

Corsica is noted for its great biodiversity, with several endemic species found only on the island. The island is home to several plant and animal species, including the Corsican red deer, the Corsican mouflon (a sort of wild sheep), and the Corsican nuthatch (a bird species). Corsica's biodiversity is protected by its natural parks and reserves, such as the Parc Naturel Régional de Corse, which encompasses over 40% of the island.

The population of Corsica is estimated to be around 330,000 people. The island contains a blend of civilizations, with influences from Italy, France, and other Mediterranean countries. The official language is French, although Corsican, a Romance language akin to Italian, is also spoken by a considerable section of the population. Corsican culture is noted for its rich legacy, including its traditional music, cuisine, and festivals.

The economy of Corsica is mostly dependent on tourism, agriculture, and fishing. Tourism is a key economy on the island, with people attracted to its natural beauty, historic landmarks, and cultural legacy. Agriculture is also important, with Corsica noted for its production of wine, olive oil, honey, and cheese. Fishing is another important sector, with the island's waterways overflowing with diverse fish species.

The topography of Corsica is defined by its rough and mountainous terrain, gorgeous coastline, Mediterranean temperature, abundant wildlife, and distinct cultural history. Its natural beauty, ancient sites, and cultural richness make it a popular destination for tourists, while its agriculture and fishing sectors contribute to its economy. Corsica's terrain is a defining element of the island and has shaped its culture, history, and way of life.

Tourists Must Know Things Before Visiting

If you're intending to visit Corsica, there are a few things you should know to make your vacation a success.

Language: The official language of Corsica is French. However, many people also speak Corsican, which is a language closely linked to Italian. English is also spoken, especially in tourist regions. It's usually a good idea to learn a few simple words in French or Corsican to help you converse with the locals.

Weather: Corsica features a Mediterranean climate, with hot summers and moderate winters. The greatest time to visit is between May and September when the weather is nice and bright. However, be prepared for intermittent rain showers and thunderstorms, especially in the hilly parts.

Transportation: The most convenient way to navigate around Corsica is by vehicle. There are various automobile rental firms available at airports and ferry terminals. Public transit is limited, and cabs can be pricey. If you prefer to go by bus, check the schedules in advance as they might be infrequent, especially on Sundays and holidays.

Housing: Corsica provides a choice of housing alternatives, from luxury hotels to budget-friendly hostels. If you're going in peak season, it's advisable to book your accommodation in advance, especially in major tourist regions. There are also several campsites and holiday homes available for people who prefer a more independent experience.

Currency: The official currency of Corsica is the Euro. Most hotels, restaurants, and stores take credit cards, but it's always a good idea to carry some cash for smaller purchases and to tip service personnel.

Food and Drink: Corsican cuisine is a blend of French and Italian influences, with a concentration on fresh, locally-sourced ingredients. Specialties include cured meats, cheeses, and seafood meals. Corsican wine is also famous for its quality and flavor. Be sure to try the local specialties during your visit.

Outdoor Activities: Corsica is a haven for outdoor enthusiasts, with countless chances for hiking, bicycling, and water sports. The island is home to various national parks and natural reserves, where you may explore gorgeous landscapes and watch indigenous species.

Cultural Attractions: Corsica has a rich cultural legacy, with influences from both French and Italian cultures. The island is home to various historic sites and museums, including the Citadel of Calvi, the Bonifacio Citadel, and the Museum of Corsica. Be sure to tour the nearby villages and towns to discover their unique cultural traditions and customs.

Safety: Corsica is considered a safe destination for travelers. However, it's always vital to take care, especially when going alone or at night. Be mindful of your surroundings, avoid carrying big sums of cash or valuables, and keep your items near to you.

Respect Local Customs: Corsicans are proud of their culture and customs. It's crucial to demonstrate respect for local norms, especially dress rules in places of worship and modest behavior in public places. Learn a few basic phrases in French or Corsican to demonstrate your admiration for the local culture.

By following these suggestions, you may ensure a safe and happy journey to this gorgeous island in the Mediterranean.

Top Activities

Corsica is recognized for providing a wealth of physical outdoor activities for tourists to partake in. From hiking to water sports, Corsica is a refuge for adventure seekers and environment enthusiasts alike.

Hiking

One of the best ways to explore Corsica's splendor is through hiking. Corsica provides a choice of pathways for hikers, from short walks to demanding excursions, all of which give stunning views of the island's craggy coastline, mountain ranges, and lush woods.

Corsica boasts a diversified terrain that draws hikers of all skill levels. Some of the most popular paths on the island are the GR 20, Mare e Monti, and Mare a Mare. The GR 20 is one of the most demanding walks in Europe and is not suggested for beginners. It covers approximately 180 kilometers and takes around 15 days to finish. The trail traverses through high mountain passes, glacial lakes, and difficult terrain, affording breathtaking views of the island's jagged peaks and valleys. The Mare e Monti is a less tough trek that takes roughly 10 days to complete. It allows hikers the ability to discover Corsica's coastline and mountain ranges, passing through small communities and affording spectacular views of the Mediterranean Sea. The Mare a Mare is an easier trek that takes roughly 6 days to complete. It offers hikers a chance to discover Corsica's rich forests, rivers, and quaint mountain villages.

One of the best things about trekking here is the chance to appreciate the island's natural splendor up close. Corsica is home to a rich diversity of flora and fauna, including wild boars, deer, and eagles. Hikers can also see Corsica's distinctive and endemic plant species, such as the Corsican pine and the Corsican lemon tree. The island's rough shoreline offers hikers the chance to swim in crystal blue seas and explore hidden coves and beaches.

Hikers in Corsica will also have the chance to enjoy the island's rich cultural heritage. Corsica has a unique history, having been ruled by many empires and governments over the years. The island's towns and villages reflect this rich past, with influences from Italy, France, and the island's own unique culture. Hikers may discover picturesque villages, eat local cuisine, and learn about Corsica's history and culture.

When arranging a hiking vacation to Corsica, it is vital to prepare thoroughly. The island's steep topography and unpredictable weather may make hiking tough, even for experienced hikers. Hikers should ensure they have suitable gear, including sturdy hiking boots, warm clothing, and waterproof coats. It is also advisable to have a map, compass, and first aid kit.

This region offers a range of accommodation alternatives for hikers, from campsites and gites to luxury hotels. The island's gites are a popular choice for hikers, offering modest accommodation in natural settings. These guesthouses are usually located in quaint communities and offer an opportunity to meet other hikers and locals.

The island's different landscapes and routes offer something for hikers of all ability levels, and the chance to enjoy the island's natural splendor up close is truly unique. However, hikers should plan carefully and ensure they have appropriate gear and accommodation before beginning their expedition.

Beach hopping

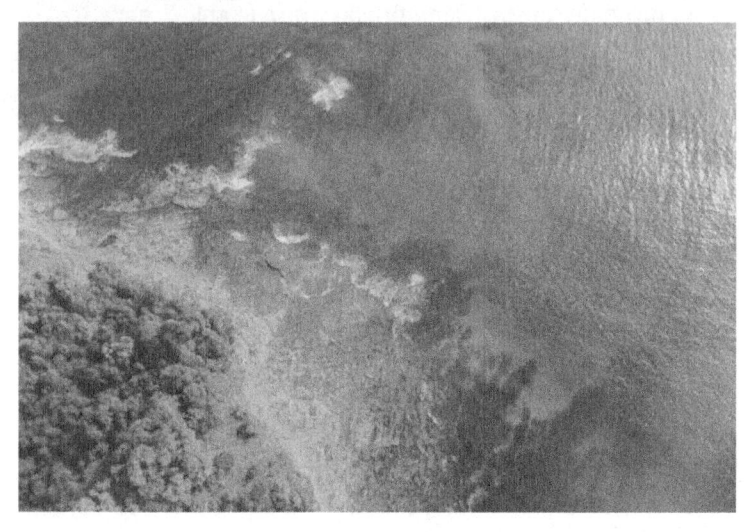

The island boasts over 1,000 kilometers of shoreline, with various beaches strewn throughout its shores. From quiet coves to huge sandy expanses, Corsica offers a diversity of beaches to explore.

One of the highlights of beach hopping here is the range of beaches that cater to different interests. For those seeking peace and serenity, the island features several hidden beaches accessible only by foot or boat. These hidden jewels provide pristine sands, blue waters, and a sense of solitude away from the crowds. Examples include Rondinara Beach, Palombaggia Beach, and Santa Giulia Beach, which are typically listed among the most beautiful beaches in the Mediterranean.

For adventure junkies, Corsica also provides unique options for beach hopping. Many beaches are tucked between stunning cliffs or surrounded by rocky terrain, giving a perfect backdrop for hiking, snorkeling, and other water activities. Calvi Beach, located on the northwest shore of the island, is recognized for its gorgeous set against the backdrop of the Citadel of Calvi. It features water sports such as paddleboarding, kayaking, and windsurfing, making it a favorite place for adventure seekers.

Corsica is also recognized for its lovely beach towns, which offer a special appeal to the beach hopping experience. Porto-Vecchio, located in the southern half of the island, is a popular coastal town that provides gorgeous beaches, such as Palombaggia and Santa Giulia, along with a busy nightlife and a selection of culinary options. Bonifacio, located on the southern tip of Corsica, is another must-visit destination famed for its stunning cliffs and magnificent beaches, notably the popular Plage de la Tonnara.

The beaches are not only famed for their natural beauty but also for their rich cultural past. Many beaches in Corsica have historical value, with vestiges of past civilizations and cultural landmarks. For example, the beach of Arone, located on the west coast of Corsica, is noted for its unusual rock formations and the Genoese Tower of Arone, a historic fortress that dates back to the 16th century. This blend of natural beauty and cultural tradition makes beach hopping in Corsica a very enriching experience.

Corsica's beaches also give a chance to indulge in the island's famed cuisine. Many beachside restaurants and cafes sell fresh seafood, local cheeses, and wines, allowing tourists to appreciate the flavors of Corsican cuisine while enjoying the breathtaking views of the Mediterranean Sea. This culinary experience adds another depth of richness to the beach-hopping vacation in Corsica.

Scuba diving

Scuba diving in Corsica is an amazing and unique activity that allows travelers to discover the pristine underwater world of this lovely Mediterranean island. Corsica boasts crystal-clear seas, diverse marine life, and magnificent underwater landscapes, making it a favorite destination for scuba diving lovers.

One of the main attractions of scuba diving in Corsica is the amazing visibility of the waters, which can reach up to 40 meters (131 feet). The crystal-clear waters offer divers unique vistas of the underwater world, including vivid coral reefs, underwater caverns, and stunning rock formations. The visibility also allows divers to view a broad assortment of marine life, including colorful fish, octopuses, groupers, and even dolphins and whales on occasion.

It is home to several renowned diving spots that cater to divers of all levels of experience. One of the most prominent dive locations is the Scandola Nature Reserve, a UNESCO World Heritage Site located on the western coast of Corsica. This protected region is recognized for its stunning cliffs, caves, and underwater canyons, which are alive with marine life. Divers can explore the vast biodiversity of the reserve, including a variety of fish species, crabs, and even the elusive Mediterranean monk seal.

Another popular diving location is the Lavezzi Islands, a series of granite islands located in the Strait of Bonifacio between Corsica and Sardinia. The Lavezzi Islands are famed for their gorgeous beaches and blue waters, as well as their abundant marine life. Divers can explore the underwater environment of the islands, which includes colorful coral gardens, swim-throughs, and encounters with schools of fish, such as barracudas, groupers, and moray eels.

For more experienced divers, the underwater caves and caverns of Corsica provide unique and fascinating diving experiences. The island is littered with various tunnels and caverns, some of which are accessible only to experienced divers. These underwater caverns are ornamented with spectacular rock formations and are typically inhabited by marine species, such as lobsters and octopuses. Diving in these caves is an adrenaline-pumping adventure for thrill-seekers and an opportunity to witness the hidden beauty of Corsica's underwater world.

When it comes to diving season, Corsica offers year-round options for scuba diving. However, the greatest time to dive in Corsica is during the summer months from May to October when the water temperature ranges from 18 to 26 degrees

Celsius (64 to 79 degrees Fahrenheit). During this time, the visibility is at its finest, and the marine life is numerous, making it an ideal time for divers to explore the underwater world of Corsica.

Whether you're a beginner or an expert diver, Corsica's underwater environment will leave you enthralled and anxious to explore more of its hidden secrets.

Canyoning

Canyoning in Corsica is an exciting and exhilarating adventure that allows people to discover the rough and gorgeous landscapes of this lovely Mediterranean island in a unique way. Corsica's crystal-clear rivers, and lush flora, make it a great destination for canyoning fans wanting an adrenaline-pumping experience in a scenic setting.

Canyoning, also known as canyoneering, involves traveling through tight gorges by lowering cliffs, jumping into pools, swimming, sliding down natural slides, and rappelling down waterfalls. It is a fascinating outdoor activity that involves physical fitness, agility, and a sense of adventure. Corsica offers a wide choice of canyoning alternatives ideal for both novices and seasoned adventurers, making it a fantastic location for all levels of skill and experience.

One of the popular canyoning places in Corsica is the Restonica Valley, located in the center of the island. The Restonica River rushes through the valley, producing a complicated network of gorges with beautiful rock formations and emerald-green pools. Canyoning in the Restonica Valley gives a unique experience of walking through tiny gorges, swimming in natural pools, and rappelling down waterfalls surrounded by lush forests and granite cliffs. The centerpiece of Restonica Valley is the Golo Canyon, which allows thrilling leaps into deep pools and rappelling down waterfalls up to 50 meters high, delivering an unforgettable trip for adrenaline addicts.

Another popular canyoning site in Corsica is the Verghellu Canyon, located in the central section of the island. The Verghellu Canyon is recognized for its beautiful landscape, with towering cliffs, turquoise pools, and small paths that demand technical abilities to negotiate. Canyoning in Verghellu Canyon entails rappelling down waterfalls, sliding down natural slides, and swimming through small gorges, giving an amazing experience for thrill-seekers.

For those seeking a more family-friendly canyoning experience, the Zoicu Canyon is a good choice. Located in the Bavella Massif, Zoicu Canyon offers a softer canyoning adventure perfect for beginners and families with children. The canyon has magnificent natural pools, tiny jumps, and easy rappels, providing a fun and exciting experience for all ages.

One of the distinctive characteristics of canyoning in Corsica is the island's clean and undisturbed natural landscape. Corsica is famed for its protected natural parks, notably the Parc Naturel Régional de Corse, which assures that the canyoning activities are conducted in an eco-friendly and sustainable manner. Canyoning guides in Corsica are well-trained and competent in navigating the canyons while protecting the delicate nature and assuring the safety of tourists.

To enjoy canyoning in Corsica to the fullest, it is vital to be prepared and equipped with the correct gear. Canyoning equipment normally comprises a wetsuit, harness, helmet, and proper boots for maneuvering slippery rocks and water. It is also vital to follow the directions of professional guides and adhere to safety regulations, as canyoning may be a physically demanding activity that requires good technique and precautions.

From navigating through tiny gorges to rappelling down waterfalls, canyoning in Corsica offers an adrenaline-pumping adventure amidst an unspoiled environment. With multiple canyoning alternatives suitable for all levels of ability and experience, Corsica is a great location for canyoning fans and thrill-seekers alike.

Rock climbing

One of the primary highlights of rock climbing in Corsica is the varied range of climbing choices available. Whether you are a beginner or an expert climber, Corsica has something to offer for everyone. The island boasts a plethora of cliffs, crags, and boulders, providing a range of climbing routes that suit to varied ability levels and inclinations. From traditional climbing to sport climbing and bouldering, Corsica offers it all.

One of the most prominent climbing sites in Corsica is the Restonica Valley. The Valley's spectacular environment with granite cliffs that rise sharply from the valley floor, providing an awe-inspiring backdrop for climbers. The climbing routes in Restonica Valley range from moderate to hard, with varied lengths and styles, making it suited for climbers of all levels. The valley also offers a wide choice of housing alternatives, from camping grounds to mountain lodges, making it a suitable base for climbers.

Another popular climbing site in Corsica is the Bavella Massif, located in the southeast half of the island. The Bavella Massif is recognized for its dramatic red granite cliffs, distinctive rock formations, and breathtaking vistas. The climbing routes in Bavella Massif are diverse, ranging from single-pitch sports routes to multi-pitch traditional routes. The area also offers a selection of bouldering chances for those who prefer this kind of climbing. Climbers can enjoy panoramic views of the Corsican environment as they ascend the cliffs, delivering a gratifying and unforgettable experience.

Apart from the breathtaking environment, rock climbing in Corsica also offers a rich cultural experience. Climbers can immerse themselves in the local culture by visiting adjacent towns, talking with people, and trying out typical Corsican foods, such as wild boar stew and chestnut soup. The island also holds different climbing events and festivals throughout the year, allowing an opportunity to meet fellow climbers and experience the local climbing community.

Safety is a primary priority in rock climbing, and Corsica offers a safe and well-maintained climbing environment. The island boasts a variety of professional local guides and climbing schools that give teaching and guidance to climbers of all levels. Additionally, Corsica has a robust climbing culture, and climbers can readily connect with other climbers for information, support, and company. However, it's crucial to always use safe climbing skills, utilize suitable gear, and be aware of local restrictions and weather conditions to ensure a safe and fun climbing experience.

River rafting

One popular sport that draws tourists from all around the world is river rafting. River rafting in Corsica offers an amazing experience for adventure lovers, with its fast-paced rivers, gorgeous scenery, and unique cultural characteristics.

Corsica boasts a number of rivers that are perfect for river rafting, including the Golo, Tavignano, and Liamone Rivers, among others. These rivers provide varied levels of difficulty, making them appropriate for both novices and expert rafters. The rivers of Corsica are characterized by their clear waters, rugged gorges, and lush foliage, creating a spectacular backdrop for an exciting journey.

One of the primary attractions of river rafting in Corsica is the adrenaline rush that comes with navigating the fast-flowing rapids. Corsica's rivers feature a combination of rapids ranging from Class II to Class IV, giving a thrilling challenge for rafters. The adrenaline-pumping rapids test the abilities and teamwork of rafters as they negotiate through twists and turns, ride over waves, and dodge hazards. River rafting in Corsica is a thrilling activity that gives a unique blend of adrenaline, adventure, and natural beauty.

River rafting also allows guests to immerse themselves in the island's rich culture and history. As rafters sail through the rivers, they pass by lovely Corsican villages perched along the banks, affording a look into the local way of life. Rafting cruises sometimes include stops in these communities, allowing guests to connect with the residents, learn about their customs and traditions, and enjoy the island's great cuisine. This cultural immersion adds a distinct and fascinating element to the river rafting experience in Corsica, making it more than just an adventure activity.

Another benefit of river rafting in Corsica is the gorgeous environment that surrounds the rivers. Rafters can enjoy beautiful views of Corsica's landscapes as they navigate through the rapids, with great opportunities for photography and appreciation of the island's unique flora and fauna. The combination of dangerous rapids and breathtaking surroundings produces an amazing experience for guests seeking an adventure in nature.

To provide a safe and enjoyable experience, river rafting in Corsica is often guided by trained instructors who provide instructions on rafting methods, safety precautions, and equipment usage. Rafting vacations are frequently planned in small groups, providing customized attention and direction. Most rafting operators supply all the essential equipment, including wetsuits, helmets, life jackets, and paddles, ensuring that tourists enjoy a safe and comfortable experience on the water.

Horseback riding

One of the joys of horseback riding in Corsica is the possibility to traverse the island's different topography. Corsica's spectacular mountain ranges, including the rough peaks of the Corsican Alps and the famed GR20 hiking trail we describe in the hiking section. Riding on horseback allows tourists to venture into these distant and awe-inspiring environments, passing through deep forests, traversing rocky hills, and crossing clear mountain streams. The panoramic views from the mountain routes are just spectacular, with vistas of green valleys, snow-capped summits, and the shimmering Mediterranean Sea stretching out in the distance.

Corsica is also home to numerous gorgeous beaches, and horseback riding along the seashore is a fantastic experience. Riding along the gorgeous sandy beaches with the turquoise seas of the Mediterranean lapping at the hooves of your horse is a wonderful treat. Tourists can experience the feeling of freedom and connection with nature as they ride down the coast, finding hidden coves, galloping through shallow waves, and basking in the sun on isolated beaches. Corsica's beaches are frequently less congested than those in other Mediterranean destinations, allowing for a calm and tranquil riding experience by the sea.

The island is noted for its old settlements located on hilltops, where time appears to have stood still. Riding through these old villages affords an insight into Corsica's past, with their tiny cobblestone alleys, antique stone buildings, and medieval churches. The residents, known as Corsicans, are proud of their unique culture and are noted for their friendly welcome toward tourists. Riding through these communities on horseback allows travelers to engage with the people, learn about Corsican traditions, and eat local cuisines, such as the famed Corsican charcuterie and cheese.

When it comes to horseback riding in Corsica, travelers have a number of options to suit their preferences and riding abilities. Many tour providers offer guided trail rides for beginners, intermediate riders, and expert equestrians. Riding itineraries can be modified to appeal to diverse interests, from leisurely rides through vineyards and olive groves to more demanding excursions in the highlands. Some excursions also include overnight stays in traditional Corsican accommodations, such as mountain refuges or rural guesthouses, providing an immersive and authentic experience of Corsican culture and lifestyle.

As with any outdoor sport, safety is a necessity during horseback riding in Corsica. Tourists are often provided with well-trained horses, suitable riding gear, and expert guides who are informed about the area's terrain and conditions. It's crucial to obey the directions of the guides and respect the natural environment, including local flora and fauna, as well as any cultural or historical monuments along the riding routes.

Mountain biking

Corsica, an ideal Mediterranean island famed for its magnificent scenery and rich cultural legacy, provides an exciting journey for mountain bike aficionados. With its varied terrain, ranging from steep mountains to lush woods and clean coastlines, Corsica is an ideal playground for mountain bike fans wanting an adrenaline-pumping adventure in a stunning natural setting.

One of the primary attractions of mountain biking in Corsica is its hard and varied terrain that caters to different ability levels. From moderate gravel routes for novices to difficult singletracks for expert bikers, Corsica has it all. The island features an enormous network of well-maintained routes that cross its different terrain, allowing a wide selection of alternatives for riders to explore.

The mountain bike paths in Corsica are renowned for their magnificent landscapes. As cyclists pedal through deep forests, they are given panoramic vistas of the shimmering Mediterranean Sea, craggy cliffs, and lovely settlements perched on hilltops. The island's various landscapes create a visual feast, with ever-changing scenery that adds to the exhilaration of the trip.

Corsica is also noted for its warm and inviting native culture. Along the mountain biking paths, riders can visit historic Corsican villages where they can pause and immerse themselves in the local way of life. With its distinctive blend of Italian and French influences, Corsican culture is distinct and gives a fascinating glimpse into the island's history and traditions.

One of the most iconic mountain bike routes in Corsica is the GR20, extending for over 180 kilometers, the GR20 spans Corsica from north to south, taking riders over steep mountain passes, rocky landscapes, and magnificent alpine vistas. The GR20 offers an unequaled adventure for seasoned riders who are eager for a thrilling and physically demanding encounter.

For those seeking a more leisurely mountain riding experience, Corsica provides plenty of possibilities as well. The island is crisscrossed with a network of gravel roads and forest tracks that are great for leisurely rides. These trails often wind through magnificent vineyards, olive groves, and chestnut forests, providing cyclists an opportunity to absorb the island's natural beauty at a more leisurely pace.

Safety is an important factor when mountain riding in Corsica. Riders should be well-prepared and equipped with suitable gear, including helmets, gloves, and knee pads. The terrain in

Corsica can be tough and technical, and riders need to be proficient and experienced to conquer the trails safely. It's also crucial to be aware of local legislation and preserve the environment by keeping on approved routes and leaving no trace.

Corsica has great infrastructure for mountain biking aficionados, with a choice of services and facilities to help riders. There are various bike rental shops and tour companies that provide equipment, guided excursions, and maps for cyclists to explore the trails. Many of the paths are well-marked, making navigating reasonably uncomplicated.

Sea kayaking

With its crystal-clear waters, quiet coves, and towering cliffs, Corsica provides an exceptional sea kayaking experience for those wanting an energetic and unique way to explore its coastline.

One of the great draws of sea kayaking in Corsica is the ability to discover its quiet coves and hidden beaches that are only accessible by water. Paddling along the tranquil waters of the Mediterranean, travelers can explore scenic bays, caves, and rock formations, while enjoying the stunning scenery and the serenity of the sea. The transparency of the seas also provides a rare opportunity for snorkeling or diving to see the diverse marine life that inhabits the region, including colorful fish, octopuses, and sea turtles.

Corsica's coastline is also defined by magnificent cliffs and rock formations that make a dramatic scene to paddle across. From the towering Calanche de Piana to the famed Bonifacio cliffs, sea kayakers may experience the breathtaking grandeur of these natural attractions from a close-up perspective. These cliffs also present exciting prospects for adventure enthusiasts, as some guided trips provide the possibility to explore sea caves, cliff jump, or even try deep-water soloing, a thrilling sort of rock climbing directly from the kayak.

For those searching for a multi-day experience, Corsica offers many sea kayaking routes that allow travelers to explore different sections of the island. One famous route is the Cap Corse, a wild and mountainous peninsula in the north of Corsica that offers a mix of tough paddling and spectacular views, including picturesque fishing villages and secluded beaches. Another alternative is the Gulf of Porto, a UNESCO World Heritage site that contains the Calanche de Piana and the Scandola Nature Reserve, noted for their extraordinary beauty and unusual rock formations.

kayaking in Corsica is also ideal for all levels of skill, from beginners to seasoned paddlers. Guided tours and rental alternatives are available, with expert guides providing safety instructions and coaching on paddling methods. Some excursions also include camping or housing alternatives, allowing travelers to immerse themselves in the natural beauty of Corsica while enjoying the adventure of sea kayaking.

Kayaking also offers opportunities to learn about the island's rich history and culture. Along the shoreline, kayakers can explore historical Genoese towers, quaint fishing communities, and historic landmarks, affording insights into Corsica's interesting past. Furthermore, meeting with the friendly inhabitants and experiencing the great Corsican cuisine, which includes seafood, charcuterie, and local wines, adds a cultural component to the sea kayaking experience.

Paragliding

This popular adventure activity lets travelers soar through the skies and take in panoramic views of Corsica's natural treasures from a birds-eye perspective. From the craggy mountains to the gorgeous beaches, paragliding in Corsica offers a remarkable and comprehensive sensory experience.

One of the ideal spots for paragliding in Corsica is the region of Porto-Vecchio. Nestled between the sea and the mountains, Porto-Vecchio offers a perfect launching site for paragliders to take flight. As you soar into the air, you'll be treated to spectacular sights of the azure Mediterranean Sea, the golden sandy beaches, and the lush greenery of Corsica's woods. The juxtaposition of the deep blue sea against the verdant terrain provides a visual extravaganza that will leave you in wonder.

Paragliding in Corsica is not just about the breathtaking scenery, but also the adrenaline-pumping pleasure of flying. As you launch into the air, you'll experience a burst of excitement as you glide over the skies, feeling weightless and free like a bird. The sense of flying, without the necessity for a motorized aircraft, is incredibly liberating and allows you to see Corsica's beauty in a unique and thrilling way.

Corsica's diverse landscape offers a variety of paragliding experiences suitable for all ability levels, from novices to expert paragliders. For beginners, tandem paragliding is a popular option, where you can fly with a skilled pilot who handles the aircraft while you enjoy the view. This allows you to experience the thrill of paragliding without the need for any prior expertise or training. More experienced paragliders can opt for solo flights, where they can push themselves by managing the air currents and exploring Corsica's breathtaking landscapes at their own pace.

One of the most popular paragliding places in Corsica is the Col de Bavella, located in the center of the island. This mountain pass offers stunning views of Corsica's iconic granite peaks, steep cliffs, and deep forests. The launch point is accessible by road, and once you're in the air, you'll be rewarded with an awe-inspiring panoramic view of Corsica's natural splendor. The Col de Bavella is also noted for its thermals, which are upward air currents that paragliders can use to gain height and lengthen their flight time, making it a paradise for skilled paragliders.

Another stunning place for paragliding in Corsica is the Gulf of Porto, a UNESCO World Heritage site noted for its dramatic red cliffs and crystal-clear waters. The launch place is positioned atop the cliffs, allowing a spectacular take-off with the azure water below. As you soar above the Gulf of Porto, you'll be rewarded with stunning views of the Calanques de Piana, a series of majestic rock formations rising from the sea, and the Scandola Nature Reserve, a pristine marine reserve alive with rich species.

Safety is of essential concern in paragliding, and Corsica has a well-established network of professional paragliding schools and instructors that adhere to stringent safety regulations. Before taking to the skies, you'll receive full training on paragliding methods, safety protocols, and weather conditions to ensure a safe and pleasurable trip.

Dialects and Language

Corsica, a lovely island located in the Mediterranean Sea, is noted not only for its stunning landscapes but also for its rich linguistic legacy. The dialects and language of Corsica are unique and represent the island's complicated history and cultural diversity.

Corsican, often known as Corsu or Lingua Corsa, is the predominant language spoken in Corsica. It belongs to the Italo-Dalmatian group of Romance languages and is strongly connected to Italian and Tuscan dialects. Corsican has two primary dialects: Northern Corsican, spoken in the northern half of the island, and Southern Corsican, spoken in the southern part. These dialects contain some variances in pronunciation, vocabulary, and syntax, but they are mutually intelligible.

Corsican has a rich oral heritage, with a vast collection of folklore, poetry, and songs that have been passed down through generations. Music is an important aspect of Corsican culture, and traditional Corsican polyphonic singing, known as paghjella, is classified as a UNESCO Intangible Cultural Heritage. Corsican language and culture have also been preserved through several Corsican language revival initiatives that promote the use of the language in schools, media, and daily life.

Corsican has been affected by several languages throughout history, notably Italian, French, and Ligurian. During the Genoese and Pisan hegemony in the Middle Ages, Corsican absorbed several Italian loanwords and adopted Italian-influenced phonetic characteristics. In the 18th century, the

French language started to acquire significance in Corsica after it was ceded to France, and French became the official language of the island during the French Revolution. As a result, Corsican witnessed a loss in usage, especially in written form, and French became the dominant language of administration, education, and media.

Today, Corsican is considered a minority language, and its usage has diminished over the years. However, efforts have been undertaken to revitalize and promote the Corsican language. Corsican is taught in schools as a regional language, and there are Corsican-language newspapers, radio stations, and websites. Corsican is also used in local administration and has official status within the scope of the European Charter for Regional or Minority Languages.

There are several regional languages and dialects spoken in Corsica, which reflect the island's cultural diversity. One of them is Gallurese, spoken in the northern half of Corsica and in the neighboring province of Gallura in Sardinia, Italy. Gallurese is a Romance language strongly linked to Corsican and Sardinian, and it shares many characteristics with Northern Corsican. Another regional language spoken in Corsica is Ligurian, which is spoken in some coastal sections of the island, especially in the province of Bonifacio.

Despite confronting problems and loss in usage, attempts have been made to resuscitate and promote Corsican as a minority language. Corsica is also home to several regional languages and dialects, such as Gallurese and Ligurian, which represent the island's cultural diversity and linguistic richness. The preservation and promotion of the dialects and language of Corsica contribute to the island's unique cultural character and legacy.

Weather

When planning a vacation to Corsica, it's crucial to understand the weather patterns that might drastically influence your experience. Corsica has a Mediterranean climate with moderate, wet winters and scorching, dry summers. The island's weather can vary based on the season, location, and height.

Winter in Corsica, which lasts from December to February, can be chilly and damp, especially in the higher mountain regions. Temperatures can range from 8°C to 14°C, with occasional rain and snowfall in the highlands. The coastal areas tend to be milder, with temperatures averaging approximately 12°C to 16°C. While winter may not be the best time for beach activities, it can be an ideal time for hikers and nature enthusiasts to explore Corsica's gorgeous trails, as the island's landscapes transform into a lush green wonderland.

As spring arrives in Corsica from March to May, the weather begins to warm up, and the island bursts into brilliant colors with flowering flowers. Temperatures can range from 12°C to 20°C, making it a lovely time to visit. Spring is a perfect time to explore Corsica's lovely villages, visit historical monuments, and enjoy outdoor activities such as hiking, cycling, and water sports.

Summer in Corsica, from June to August, is the busiest tourist season when the island has its hottest and driest weather. Temperatures can climb up to 30°C or greater, especially in coastal areas. The sea is warm and welcoming, great for swimming, snorkeling, and other aquatic activities. The long days and warm evenings make it a great time for beach lovers, sunbathers, and those who want to partake in water sports or simply rest by the sea. However, do note that popular tourist locations can get congested during this season, and lodging prices may be higher.

Autumn in Corsica, from September to November, is another fantastic time to come as the weather is moderate and the tourist throngs begin to drop out. Temperatures range from 15°C to 23°C, making it comfortable for outdoor activities. The fall foliage in Corsica's woodlands is a sight to behold, with leaves changing to vivid colors of red, orange, and yellow. Autumn is a terrific time for wine connoisseurs as Corsica's vineyards are in full swing with the harvest season, allowing opportunities for wine tasting and cultural excursions.

It's crucial to know that Corsica's weather can vary depending on the location and altitude. The coastal regions tend to be warmer and drier, whereas the interior and hilly parts might be cooler and wetter. Corsica's microclimates also make it possible to experience different weather patterns in a single day, with bright mornings, gloomy afternoons, and occasional rain showers.

In conclusion, Corsica's weather is Mediterranean, with moderate, rainy winters and scorching, dry summers. Spring and autumn are the best periods to visit for pleasant weather and fewer crowds, while summer is perfect for beach and water activities. Winter can be chilly and damp, but great for hikers and nature enthusiasts. Regardless of the season, Corsica's landscapes, cultural heritage, and gorgeous beaches make it a year-round destination worth exploring. Make sure to check the weather forecast and pack accordingly to fully enjoy your trip to this beautiful island.

Getting Here

If you're considering a trip to Corsica, it's crucial to understand how to get there. In this thorough explanation, we'll examine the many choices for arriving in Corsica, including by flight, ferry, and by automobile.

By Air: Corsica has many airports that serve as entrance points for travelers. The two main airports on the island are Bastia-Poretta Airport and Ajaccio Napoleon Bonaparte Airport. These airports are well-connected to major cities in France, as well as other European locations, with regular flights offered by major airlines and low-cost carriers.

Bastia-Poretta Airport is located on the northeastern side of Corsica, near the town of Bastia, and serves as a gateway to the northern section of the island. Ajaccio Napoleon Bonaparte Airport, on the other hand, is situated on the western coast of Corsica, near the capital city of Ajaccio, and gives access to the southern and western portions of the island.

Traveling by air to Corsica is convenient and time-saving, with trip lengths varied based on the departure place. It's suggested to book flights in advance, especially during the high summer season, as availability may be restricted and prices can increase closer to the travel dates.

By Ferry: Another popular route to arrive in Corsica is by ferry. Corsica is well-connected to mainland France and Italy by ferry services that run from numerous ports. Major ferry ports in Corsica include Bastia, Ajaccio, Calvi, and Porto Vecchio, among others.

Ferry services are operated by many businesses, giving both passenger and vehicle transit alternatives. Traveling by ferry allows you to bring your own vehicle, which can be helpful if you plan to explore Corsica on your own. However, ferry travel can be time-consuming, with journey lengths ranging from a few hours to overnight crossings, depending on the route and the provider.

Ferry tickets can be purchased in advance or at the port, but it's encouraged to reserve in advance during the busy season since availability can be restricted. It's also vital to examine the ferry schedules and routes, as they may vary based on the season and weather conditions.

By Automobile: If you're intending to tour Corsica by automobile, you have the choice to drive from mainland France or Italy. Corsica is connected to mainland France by ferries that operate from ports such as Nice, Toulon, and Marseille. The ferry ride takes many hours, and you can bring your vehicle onboard to tour the island on your own time.

Alternatively, you may also reach Corsica by automobile from Italy through ferries that operate from ports such as Livorno, Genoa, and Savona. These ferries offer choices for both passenger and car transportation, providing a handy alternative to travel to Corsica with your own vehicle.

When driving to Corsica, it's necessary to be prepared for the journey, as it requires crossing the sea on a ferry. It's essential to reserve ferry tickets in advance, prepare for the driving routes and check the ferry schedules, and ensure that you have all the appropriate documentation for your vehicle, including insurance and registration papers.

Each form of transportation has its own advantages and considerations, such as convenience, trip duration, and the opportunity to bring your own vehicle. It's vital to plan and book in advance, especially during the high season, to ensure a smooth and comfortable voyage to this lovely Mediterranean island.

Top Attractions

With its diversified landscapes, stunning beaches, historic ruins, and picturesque villages, Corsica provides a wide selection of tourist attractions that cater to different interests.

Calvi Citadel

The Calvi Citadel in Corsica is a beautiful ancient fortification that rests majestically atop a rocky slope overlooking the Mediterranean Sea. Located in the town of Calvi on the northwestern coast of Corsica, a picturesque island in the Mediterranean Sea, the Calvi Citadel is a must-visit location for history aficionados, architecture admirers, and nature lovers alike.

The Calvi Citadel, also known as the "Citadelle de Calvi" in French, is a well-preserved citadel that dates back to the 13th century. It was erected by the Genoese, who controlled over Corsica during that period and acted as a crucial military bastion to protect the town of Calvi and its harbor from intruders. The fortress has a rich history, having been conquered and inhabited by numerous nations over the years, notably the Genoese, the French, and the British. Today, it stands as a remarkable witness to Corsica's stormy past.

The Citadel is notable for its spectacular fortifications and defensive walls, which encircle the entire stronghold. The walls are composed of native pink granite and are embellished with massive ramparts, bastions, and towers. The Citadel's strategic location on a hill affords panoramic views of the surrounding area, including the blue waves of the Mediterranean Sea, the red roofs of Calvi town, and the magnificent mountains in the distance. The views from the Citadel are incredibly magnificent, making it a favorite site for photography and taking in the natural beauty of Corsica.

Within the Citadel, tourists can explore the small winding lanes, picturesque alleys, and historic structures that make up this medieval fortification. One of the attractions of the Citadel is the Saint-Jean-Baptiste Cathedral, a stunning 13th-century cathedral with a remarkable pink granite front and a baroque interior. The cathedral is still in operation today and offers visitors a look into the religious history of the region. There are also various museums and exhibitions within the Citadel, notably the Museum of Corsican Ethnography, which showcases the island's cultural heritage and traditions.

The Citadel also offers lots of natural beauty. The fortress is surrounded by luxuriant flora, including aromatic Mediterranean shrubs, wildflowers, and ancient olive trees. The combination of history, architecture, and natural beauty makes the Calvi Citadel a unique and compelling attraction for travelers.

Visiting the Citadel is a voyage back in time, where visitors may immerse themselves in the rich history and culture of Corsica. Walking along the historic walls, exploring the small lanes, and taking in the panoramic vistas are experiences that transport visitors to a bygone period. The Citadel also holds many cultural events and performances throughout the year, including music concerts, art exhibitions, and historical reenactments, contributing to its colorful ambiance.

To truly appreciate Calvi Citadel, it is suggested to take a guided tour or rent an audio guide since they provide insights into the history and significance of the castle. The Citadel is open to tourists year-round, however, some areas may be closed during the low season. Admission costs may apply, but the experience of touring this wonderful historical monument is well worth it.

Bonifacio

This magnificent town is recognized for its breathtaking limestone cliffs, blue waters, and medieval buildings, making it a unique and captivating destination for travelers seeking natural beauty and cultural legacy.

One of the main attractions of Bonifacio is its spectacular limestone cliffs, which offer an amazing backdrop to the town. These towering cliffs, known as the "White Cliffs of Bonifacio," are constructed of pure white limestone that has been eroded by the sea and wind over millions of years, resulting in stunning cliffs that overlook the Mediterranean Sea. These cliffs are a sight to behold, and visitors may explore them by taking a boat tour or trekking along the cliff paths to enjoy panoramic views of the sea and the town.

It is also noted for its crystal-clear turquoise waters. The town is encircled by the Mediterranean Sea, and its shoreline is filled with lovely beaches, coves, and inlets that give chances for swimming, snorkeling, and diving. One of the most famous beaches in Bonifacio is Plage de Sperone, a pristine sandy beach with turquoise waves that is regarded as one of the most beautiful beaches in Corsica. Visitors can relax on the soft beach, have a relaxing dip in the beautiful seas, or explore the neighboring marine life by snorkeling or diving.

Bonifacio is also noted for its rich history and medieval architecture. The town is set on a cliff overlooking the sea, and its narrow alleys are studded with well-preserved medieval buildings, fortifications, and churches that are a monument to its past. The Citadel of Bonifacio, a castle built in the 9th century, is a significant landmark in the town and gives spectacular views of the sea and the surrounding landscape. The Staircase of the King of Aragon, a steep flight of stairs built into the cliff, is another notable site in Bonifacio that offers panoramic views of the town and the sea.

Bonifacio is likewise a bustling and lovely town with a lively vibe. The town is recognized for its native cuisine, which combines Mediterranean and Corsican flavors to create delectable meals that are a treat for food lovers. Visitors can luxuriate in fresh seafood, local cheeses, charcuterie, and other delights at the several restaurants, cafes, and marketplaces in the town. The town also hosts different cultural events, including music festivals, art exhibitions, and traditional celebrations, which offer an insight into the local culture and traditions.

In terms of outdoor activities, Bonifacio offers a wide selection of options for travelers. Apart from visiting the cliffs and beaches, travelers can also take boat journeys to the adjacent Lavezzi Islands, a series of small granite islands with crystal-clear waters and exquisite beaches. These islands are part of a protected marine reserve and are noted for their rich marine life, making them a popular destination for snorkeling and diving. Additionally, visitors can trek along the coastal paths, rent kayaks or paddleboards to explore the sea caves and grottos or go on a sailing expedition to discover the hidden beauties of the Corsican coast.

Scandola Nature Reserve

Scandola Nature Reserve is a beautiful UNESCO World Heritage site that combines awe-inspiring vistas, abundant wildlife, and unique cultural value. Spread over an area of 9000 hectares, this natural gem is a must-visit location for nature lovers and adventure enthusiasts alike.

Nestled on the western coast of Corsica, Scandola Nature Reserve is recognized for its stunning cliffs, towering red rock formations, and crystal-clear blue waters. The reserve is called after the Scandola Peninsula, which is the center of the reserve and is made up of rocky cliffs that rise dramatically from the sea, forming a spectacular background against the horizon.

One of the features of Scandola Nature Reserve is its diverse and prolific aquatic life. The reserve is home to a large assortment of fish species, dolphins, whales, and seals, making it a prime place for snorkeling, diving, and animal watching. The underwater environment of Scandola is a stunning sight, with bright corals, sponges, and other marine flora and fauna thriving in the pure waters.

The peculiar geology of Scandola Nature Reserve is also a sight to behold. The red sandstone cliffs, sculpted by erosion and weathering over millions of years, offer a spectacular display of geological formations, including caves, arches, and towering stacks. The juxtaposition of the red cliffs against the turquoise blue of the Mediterranean Sea creates a bizarre and awe-inspiring landscape that is really unforgettable.

Scandola Nature Reserve is not just a haven for natural beauty, but it also contains a cultural value. The reserve is home to notable cultural heritage sites, including old Genoese towers that were built during the 16th century to guard against pirates. These antique towers stand as a tribute to Corsica's rich past and give a unique touch to the landscape of the reserve.

Exploring Scandola Nature Reserve is an adventure in itself. Visitors can take boat tours that allow them to sail around the coastline, marvel at the spectacular cliffs, and see the plentiful animals. Hiking routes also allow possibilities for intrepid travelers to explore the area on foot, affording breathtaking panoramic views of the craggy coastline and the turquoise waters below. It's crucial to note that access to specific portions of the reserve may be restricted to protect the fragile environment and preserve its natural beauty.

As a UNESCO World Heritage site, Scandola Nature Reserve is dedicated to protecting its unique habitats and maintaining its ecological balance. The reserve is strictly protected, and visitors are obliged to adopt responsible tourist practices, such as not disturbing wildlife, avoiding littering, and staying on authorized pathways. This assures that future generations can continue to appreciate the unspoiled splendor of this natural gem.

Corte

Corte is a historic and cultural gem that is rich in natural beauty, steeped in history, and home to a vibrant local culture. In this thorough explanation, we will delve into the many characteristics that make Corte a must-visit site for tourists.

Corte holds a prominent place in Corsican history. It was the capital of Corsica during the island's brief time of independence in the 18th century, and it remains a significant symbol of Corsican nationalism. The town's historic core is dominated by the towering fortress-like citadel, which was erected by the Genoese in the 15th century and later served as the residence of Corsican leaders.

The Museum of Corsica, located within the citadel, provides a unique glimpse into the island's history and culture. It showcases relics, artwork, and documents that illustrate Corsican customs, folklore, and way of life. The museum also exhibits an excellent collection of Corsican musical instruments, highlighting the island's rich musical tradition.

One of the unique cultural elements of Corte is its language. Corsican, a Romance language, is commonly spoken in the town, and hearing the inhabitants speak Corsican adds to the true experience of visiting Corte. The town's residents take pleasure in their Corsican identity, and tourists may experience the colorful local culture through its language, cuisine, and traditions.

Surrounded by towering mountains, Corte is noted for its stunning natural beauty. The town is situated in the middle of the Corsican mountains, giving it a suitable location for adventure enthusiasts. The adjacent Restonica Valley is a treasure for hikers, with its rough environment, crystal-clear rivers, and magnificent routes that lead to pristine mountain lakes. The Tavignano River, which runs through the town, offers chances for swimming and other water activities throughout the warmer months.

Corte is also home to the stunning Gorges de la Restonica, a tiny canyon with high cliffs and blue ponds. This natural wonder is a must-visit for nature enthusiasts and adventure seekers, who may explore the gorges on foot or by kayak, and marvel at the stunning surroundings.

Corsican cuisine is renowned for its robust and savory dishes, and Corte is no exception. The town's restaurants and cafes give up typical Corsican gastronomy that is a pleasure for the taste senses. Local specialties include wild boar stew, brocciu (Corsican cheese made from ewe's milk), and figatellu (Corsican pork sausage). The town's weekly farmers' market offers a chance to try and purchase local food, such as honey, chestnuts, and olive oil.

Corte features various colorful festivals and events throughout the year that exhibit the town's rich cultural past. The Fiera di u Casgiu, held yearly in April, honors Corsican cheese with tastings, demonstrations, and competitions. The Fête de la Musique, held in June, is a spectacular festival of Corsican music, with concerts and performances taking place in the streets and squares of Corte. The town also holds the Corsican National Day celebrations on July 14th, featuring parades, concerts, and other cultural activities.

Porto-Vecchio

Porto-Vecchio is a spectacular resort located on the southern shore of the beautiful island, famed for its stunning beaches, blue waters, rich history, and active culture. This charming village is a renowned tourist attraction, attracting travelers from all over the world with its unique charm and natural beauty.

Porto-Vecchio is noted for its stunning beaches, which are among the best in Corsica. The most iconic of these is Palombaggia Beach, with its pure white sand, crystal-clear waves, and attractive pine trees. It's a veritable paradise for sun worshippers and water sports fans alike, with options for swimming, snorkeling, kayaking, and more. Another must-visit beach in Santa Giulia, famed for its shallow, quiet waves that are great for families with children.

Apart from its beaches, Porto-Vecchio also provides a rich history and cultural legacy. The town's origins extend back to the 16th century, and its old town, known as "La Haute Ville," is a tangle of narrow cobblestone lanes, ancient ramparts, and antique buildings that ooze a medieval beauty. The citadel, with its towering walls and panoramic views of the Gulf of Porto-Vecchio, is a must-visit for history fans and anyone seeking stunning landscapes.

It is also recognized for its robust nightlife and eating scene. The town is littered with a wealth of cafes, pubs, and restaurants that provide a wide variety of cuisines, ranging from local Corsican specialties to worldwide dishes. The marina is also a popular destination for a leisurely promenade, with its magnificent ships, boutique stores, and bustling atmosphere.

Nature enthusiasts will find lots to explore in and around Porto-Vecchio. The surrounding Corsican Mountains offer chances for climbing and trekking, with trails that lead to stunning landscapes and natural treasures such as the Ospedale Forest and the Bavella Needles. Boat cruises are also offered, taking visitors on excursions to discover the scenic coastline, secluded coves, and remote islands that dot the blue seas of the Mediterranean Sea.

For people interested in cultural activities, Porto-Vecchio presents a range of events and festivals throughout the year. The Bastille Day events in July involve fireworks, music, and dancing, while the Porto-Vecchio Music Festival in September presents local and international performers in a lively atmosphere. The town also conducts markets where visitors can experience local items such as cheeses, cured meats, and wines, which are all vital aspects of Corsican gastronomy.

Accommodation options in Porto-Vecchio are many, ranging from opulent resorts to modest guesthouses and vacation rentals. Many of these lodgings provide spectacular views of the Mediterranean Sea, and some are located within walking distance of the beaches and the old town. It's crucial to remember that booking in advance is suggested, especially during the high summer season, as Porto-Vecchio is a popular tourist destination.

Aiguilles de Bavella

Situated in the heart of the Corsican highlands, Aiguilles de Bavella is a series of remarkable granite peaks that rise magnificently from the surrounding valleys, providing a beautiful view that attracts travelers from all over the world.

The Aiguilles de Bavella is a group of needle-like spires that reach heights of up to 1,218 meters (3,996 ft) above sea level. These massive rock formations are the consequence of millions of years of erosion, which have molded the granite into its unique and distinctive shapes. The contrast between the high peaks and the verdant valleys below creates a stunning and awe-inspiring landscape that is a feast for the eyes.

One of the finest ways to explore the beauty of Aiguilles de Bavella is through trekking in the surrounding area. There are several trails that offer varied levels of difficulty, ranging from short walks to tough hikes for expert hikers. The most famous trail is the GR20, which is considered one of the most demanding long-distance hiking trails in Europe. The GR20 passes into the heart of the Corsican highlands, including the Aiguilles de Bavella, and offers stunning views of the rocky peaks, deep valleys, and lush woods that make up this unspoiled wilderness.

For rock climbers, Aiguilles de Bavella is also a popular location. The granite summits offer a variety of climbing routes for different skill levels, ranging from beginner-friendly to advanced. Climbers can challenge themselves with multi-pitch routes that require technical abilities and offer amazing views from the summit of the spires. However, climbing in Aiguilles de Bavella demands experience and appropriate equipment, and climbers should always exercise caution and follow safety requirements.

Aiguilles de Bavella also offers additional recreational activities. The landscape is lined with crystal-clear rivers and natural pools, which are great for swimming and relaxing during the hot summer months. Canyoning is also a popular sport in the region, allowing people to explore the deep gorges and ravines made by the rivers, and indulge in thrilling experiences such as rappelling and leaping into natural pools.

The Aiguilles de Bavella area is also home to significant biodiversity, with a variety of flora and fauna that flourish in this pure setting. Pine forests, maquis shrublands, and wildflowers dot the landscape, providing habitat for rare and endemic species. Wildlife aficionados can view species such as mouflons (wild sheep), golden eagles, and peregrine falcons, among others. The area is particularly famed for its Corsican pigs, which are known for their unusual appearance and are a part of the local culture.

For those who want to immerse themselves in the local culture, Aiguilles de Bavella also offers possibilities to sample Corsican traditions and food. There are tiny towns nearby where visitors may engage with the friendly residents, learn about their way of life, and sample wonderful Corsican specialties such as charcuterie, cheeses, and honey. Local festivals and events showcase Corsican music, dance, and crafts, providing a look into the rich cultural past of the island.

Palombaggia Beach

Renowned for its crystal-clear turquoise waters, powdery white sands, and magnificent natural landscape, Palombaggia Beach is a veritable paradise for beach lovers and nature enthusiasts alike.

The beach is easily accessible from the surrounding town of Porto-Vecchio, which is just a short drive away. Visitors can either rent a car or take a taxi to reach Palombaggia Beach. Upon arrival, tourists are welcomed by a breathtaking view of azure waves softly lapping against the shore, with grassy hills and dense pine forests providing a backdrop.

One of the most prominent qualities of Palombaggia Beach is its fine white sand, which feels wonderfully soft and powdery to the touch. The sand is made up of microscopic bits of crushed shells, giving it a unique texture and a dazzlingly bright look. Walking barefoot down the beach is a sensory delight, as the fine sand gently rubs your feet with each step.

The water at Palombaggia Beach is very pure and has a lovely blue tint that is distinctive of the Mediterranean Sea. The tranquil seas are great for swimming, and guests may also enjoy numerous water activities such as snorkeling, paddle boarding, and kayaking. The beach descends gently into the water, making it safe for swimmers of all ages and abilities.

Palombaggia Beach is bordered by the magnificent scenery of jagged granite boulders, pine trees, and maquis shrubland. The maquis, which is a rich Mediterranean flora consisting of aromatic herbs and wildflowers, fills the air with delicious perfume, adding to the sensory experience of the beach. The aroma of the maquis combining with the salty sea breeze is a unique and unforgettable sensory experience.

There are various services accessible at Palombaggia Beach, including sun loungers and umbrellas for rent, as well as showers and toilets for public use. There are also various coastal restaurants and cafes where guests may delight in great local cuisine, including as fresh seafood and Corsican specialties. Picnic spots are also provided for individuals who like to bring their own meals.

Palombaggia Beach is not only a beautiful natural beauty but it is also noted for its eco-friendly operations. The beach is a protected area, and efforts have been undertaken to preserve its pristine condition. Visitors are encouraged to follow the "Leave No Trace" principles, which promote responsible tourism and environmental conservation.

Filitosa

Nestled amidst the rugged environment of Corsica, a lovely island in the Mediterranean Sea, is Filitosa, an old archaeological site that provides a window into the island's prehistoric past. Filitosa is a must-visit place for history enthusiasts and those interested in archaeology and anthropology.

Located near the village of Sollacaro in southwestern Corsica, Filitosa is noted for its magnificent collection of megalithic sculptures and constructions that date back to the Neolithic period, circa 3300-1500 BCE. The site was discovered in the 1940s and has since been intensively examined, offering unique insights into the ancient societies that formerly inhabited Corsica.

One of the features of Filitosa is its unique collection of menhirs, which are enormous, standing stones carved with complex human faces and weapons. These sculptures, some reaching up to 2.5 meters in height, are thought to portray warriors and are a unique feature of Filitosa. The amount of detail and craftsmanship in these statues is awe-inspiring, reflecting the artistic and technical skills of the ancient inhabitants of Corsica.

The site also has additional megalithic constructions, including alignments of menhirs, dolmens (stone graves), and circular fortifications known as Torri. These constructions reveal evidence about the social and cultural behaviors of the Neolithic people who lived in Filitosa. The site's layout and the location of the megaliths suggest that Filitosa was a ceremonial and ritualistic center, likely related to ancestor worship and fertility ceremonies.

As visitors explore Filitosa, they can follow the well-marked trails that weave around the site, allowing them to investigate the numerous features and constructions in their own time. Informational panels provide insights into the history and significance of the site, making it a fascinating and instructive experience.

One of the distinctive elements of Filitosa is its interactive approach to archaeology. The site has a rebuilt village, which provides visitors with a look into the daily life of the prehistoric people. Here, visitors can observe rebuilt homes, tools, and other relics, as well as engage in demonstrations of ancient methods, such as flint knapping and pottery manufacturing. This hands-on experience offers a deeper understanding of the daily lives and technological accomplishments of the Neolithic people.

Filitosa also has a museum that contains an outstanding collection of items, including pottery, tools, and weaponry, uncovered at the site. These items provide fresh insights into the ancient culture of Filitosa, shedding light on the tools, weapons, and technology that were employed by the prehistoric inhabitants. The museum also shows the findings of archaeological investigation and provides a detailed picture of the site's significance.

Filitosa is likewise a natural wonder. The location is set in a lovely valley, surrounded by lush flora, olive groves, and vineyards, giving a stunning backdrop for tourists to explore and appreciate the beauty of Corsica's scenery.

Piana Calanches

Located on the western coast, Piana Calanches is a UNESCO World Heritage site famed for its red granite cliffs, towering peaks, and spectacular panoramic views.

The Piana Calanches are a series of rocky cliffs and rock formations that span along the coast of Corsica for roughly 10 kilometers. The red granite cliffs, eroded by wind and water over millions of years, have been molded into a variety of shapes, including sharp peaks, craggy ridges, and intricate rock formations. The outcome is a spectacular and surreal landscape that has been compared to a lunar landscape or a fantasy movie set.

One of the most notable rock formations in Piana Calanches is the "Tête de Chien" or "Dog's Head," which resembles the profile of a dog when viewed from a certain angle. Other prominent formations include the "Capu di Muru" and the

"Capu Rossu," which are tall, jagged peaks that rise spectacularly from the sea. The juxtaposition of the red granite against the azure blue of the Mediterranean Sea provides a breathtaking visual spectacle that draws visitors from around the world.

Exploring Piana Calanches is a unique experience that allows travelers to marvel at the force of nature. There are various ways to experience this natural treasure, including hiking, boating, and driving along the meandering coastal roads. Hiking routes offer a closer look at the rock formations and allow tourists to appreciate the delicate features of the area. The most famous walk is the "Sentier des Crêtes," a tough but rewarding path that gives panoramic views of the cliffs, the sea, and the surrounding landscape.

Boat trips are another popular way to experience Piana Calanches. Sailing along the coast provides a fresh perspective, allowing tourists to observe the cliffs from the ocean and appreciate their enormous scale and beauty. Some boat cruises also provide the opportunity to swim or snorkel in the crystal-clear waters of the Mediterranean, adding an extra element of adventure to the experience.

Driving around the coastal roads of Piana Calanches is also a must-do for many tourists. The winding roads give amazing vistas at every bend, with the cliffs and the sea providing a stunning backdrop. There are various viewpoints along the path where visitors can stop and take in the environment, including the "Belvédère de Capo Rosso," which gives panoramic views of the Gulf of Porto and the surrounding landscape.

Apart from its natural beauty, Piana Calanches also has cultural value. The area is home to typical Corsican villages, where visitors may immerse themselves in the local culture and learn about the history and way of life of the Corsican people. The village of Piana, in particular, is recognized for its attractive stone cottages and picturesque streets, giving it an ideal place to relax and absorb in the true Corsican ambiance.

L'Île-Rousse

L'Île-Rousse, often known as Ile de Beauté (Island of Beauty), is a lovely seaside town located on the northwest coast. This attractive destination provides guests with an amazing experience with its breathtaking landscapes, rich history, and vibrant culture.

One of the primary attractions of L'Île-Rousse is its lovely sandy beaches. The town boasts numerous magnificent beaches, including Plage de l'Ostriconi, Plage de Lozari, and Plage de Bodri, which are famed for their crystal-clear blue seas and fine golden sand. These beaches provide great settings for swimming, sunbathing, and water sports like snorkeling and kayaking. Tourists can also take leisurely strolls along the promenade, which is bordered by palm trees, and enjoy the breathtaking views of the Mediterranean Sea.

L'Île-Rousse is particularly recognized for its bustling town center. The village includes a gorgeous red granite lighthouse, which is a symbol of the town and affords panoramic views of the surrounding area. The town square, Place Paoli, is a dynamic center with its bustling market, colorful homes, and various cafes and restaurants. Tourists can experience native Corsican specialties, such as charcuterie, cheese, and wines, and immerse themselves in the warm and friendly ambiance of Corsican culture.

The town is steeped in history and has a rich tradition that is reflected in its architecture. L'Île-Rousse was founded in the 18th century by Pascal Paoli, a Corsican hero, and its streets are dotted with antique houses and monuments. One of the prominent landmarks of the town is the Church of Santa Maria, a lovely baroque church with an intricate exterior and towering bell tower. Another historical monument worth visiting is the Citadel, a 16th-century stronghold that offers panoramic views of the town and the sea.

For nature lovers, L'Île-Rousse offers plenty of chances for outdoor activities. The neighboring Agriates Desert, a designated nature reserve, is a huge wilderness with rocky terrain, clean beaches, and maquis-covered hills. Tourists can explore this unique area on foot, by bike, or by 4x4 vehicles, and marvel at its unspoiled beauty. The Scandola Nature Reserve, a UNESCO World Heritage Site, is also within reach, offering boat cruises to explore its stunning cliffs, caverns, and abundant marine life.

L'Île-Rousse is also a gateway to the rest of Corsica, allowing travelers to explore the larger island. From the town, travelers can enjoy a beautiful train trip on the Corsican Railway, known as the "Train des Agriates," which goes through breathtaking landscapes and gives panoramic views of the Corsican countryside. Nearby, the town of Calvi, with its historic fortress and gorgeous beaches, is just a short drive away. Other popular places in Corsica, such as Bastia, Porto-Vecchio, and Bonifacio, can also be readily visited from L'Île-Rousse.

Propriano

Propriano is a picturesque beach village located on the western shore as well. It is a popular destination for travelers looking to enjoy the natural beauty and culture of this French island. In this section, we will provide a thorough description of what makes Propriano a unique and intriguing site to visit.

First and foremost, Propriano features a spectacular natural environment that includes crystal-clear waters and gorgeous beaches. The hamlet is perched between two mountains and overlooks the Gulf of Valinco, giving visitors with spectacular views of the sea and surrounding surroundings. Visitors can take a stroll along the harbor and enjoy the sight of fishing boats and yachts, or venture out to the adjacent beaches to swim, sunbathe, and indulge in other water sports activities.

The town has a rich legacy that extends back to the Roman Empire, and visitors can explore historical ruins and artifacts that are still preserved in the vicinity. For example, the Church of Notre Dame de la Miséricorde is a stunning Romanesque-style church that dates back to the 12th century and is a must-visit location for history aficionados.

For people interested in art and culture, Propriano provides various museums and art galleries that highlight the works of local artists and artisans. The Filitosa Museum, for example, includes a collection of prehistoric relics and displays that shed light on the island's past history and culture.

Food fans will also find lots to enjoy in Propriano. The town features a broad selection of restaurants and cafes that provide typical Corsican food, such as grilled meat and fish, wild boar stew, and cheese created from the milk of free-ranging goats. Visitors can also enjoy local wines and liqueurs, such as the famed Muscat and Myrtle liqueur, which are made in the neighboring hills and valleys.

One of the most popular activities in Propriano is hiking. The village is bordered by mountains, valleys, and forests that offer some of the most spectacular hiking paths on the island. Visitors may explore the Corsican countryside and appreciate the natural beauty of the region, while also experiencing the island's distinctive flora and fauna.

For those seeking a more adventurous experience, Propriano provides various chances for outdoor sports, including diving, windsurfing, and sailing. The clean waters of the Gulf of Valinco provide an ideal environment for these activities, and visitors can take lessons or rent equipment from local operators.

Finally, Propriano is an excellent base for visiting the rest of Corsica. The town is strategically placed on the western shore, making it a suitable starting point for day travels to other regions of the island. Visitors can explore the adjacent cities of Sartene, Bonifacio, and Ajaccio, or venture further out to see the rugged beauty of the island's interior.

Genoese Tower

The Genoese Towers is a unique historical relic that shows the rich cultural legacy of the Mediterranean island. These towers, also known as "Torra" in the Corsican language, are strategically positioned along the coastline and serve as a reminder of Corsica's tumultuous past, its historical significance as a key trade route, and the architectural ingenuity of the Genoese Republic.

The Genoese Towers were created during the Genoese control of Corsica, which lasted from the 13th to the 18th centuries. Corsica, located in the Mediterranean Sea between France and Italy, was an important territory for its strategic location along major trade routes. The Genoese Republic, a powerful maritime state situated in modern-day Italy, aimed to dominate Corsica for its economic and strategic importance.

The Towers were built as defensive constructions to protect Corsica against invasions by rival kingdoms and marauding pirates. The towers were often placed on high cliffs overlooking the sea, providing a strategic vantage point to notice approaching dangers. The towers were also used to communicate with other towers along the coast using smoke signals during the day and bonfires at night, permitting speedy communication across large distances.

The architectural design of the Towers is outstanding, showcasing the engineering and building techniques of the time. The towers were built using local limestone and were meant to be durable and resilient against attackers. They often have a circular or square shape, with sturdy walls and thin openings for firing weapons. Some of the towers also featured drawbridges, trap doors, and other defensive elements.

Apart from their military purpose, the Towers also served as administrative hubs for the Genoese Republic. They were employed as customs posts to collect tolls from passing ships and to enforce trade laws. The towers also housed garrisons of soldiers who maintained peace and order in the region and protected the interests of the Genoese Republic.

Today, the Genoese Towers is a famous tourist destination in Corsica, enticing visitors with its historical significance and spectacular coastal views. Many of the towers have been repaired and conserved, allowing tourists to explore their interiors and learn about their intriguing history. Some of the towers also hold museums or exhibitions that provide insights into Corsica's past, especially its link with the Genoese Republic.

Visiting the Towers is not only an opportunity to enjoy its architectural splendor but also to learn about Corsica's rich history and cultural heritage. The towers provide a testament to the island's complex past, marked by centuries of political battles, trade rivalries, and military engagements. They are a monument to the creativity and resilience of the people who lived on the island during those times, and a reminder of Corsica's continuing character and individuality.

Monte d'Oro

Monte d'Oro is a beautiful mountain peak that offers breathtaking natural beauty and outdoor activity activities for tourists. Rising to an elevation of 2,389 meters (7,844 feet), Monte d'Oro is the third-highest mountain in Corsica and one of the most distinctive sights of the island. Its unusual pyramid-like shape and commanding presence make it a favorite destination for nature enthusiasts, hikers, and mountaineers.

One of the most striking qualities of Monte d'Oro is its spectacular panoramic views. From the summit, tourists are greeted with awe-inspiring vistas of Corsica's mountainous landscapes, including verdant valleys, dense forests, and sparkling rivers. On clear days, it's also possible to see the neighboring islands of Elba and Capraia in the distance. The stunning scenery makes Monte d'Oro a favored place for photographers and environment enthusiasts looking to capture the majesty of Corsica's wilderness.

For outdoor aficionados, Monte d'Oro offers a wealth of recreational activities. Hiking is the most popular pastime, with a range of trails that appeal to different levels of fitness and expertise. The GR20, runs via Monte d'Oro, providing ambitious trekkers with an opportunity to tackle this iconic mountain as part of their Corsican trip. Along the trip, hikers will meet varied landscapes, including dense woods of Corsican pine, mountainous terrain, and alpine meadows studded with brilliant wildflowers.

Monte d'Oro also offers good prospects for mountaineering and rock climbing. The mountain's granite cliffs and harsh terrain provide a tough playground for experienced climbers, with routes ranging from simple to difficult. Climbers can try their skills on steep walls, sharp peaks, and exposed faces, surrounded by the breathtaking scenery that adds to the exhilaration of the ascent.

Another attraction of Monte d'Oro is its abundant biodiversity. The mountain is part of the Corsican Regional Nature Park, a protected region that is home to a broad range of plant and animal species. As hikers and climbers make their way through the mountain, they may see Corsican mouflons, wild boars, and many bird species, including golden eagles and bearded vultures. The mountain's unique flora includes endemic species such as the Corsican pine and the Monte d'Oro violet, adding to its ecological value.

To properly appreciate the natural beauty and cultural significance of Monte d'Oro, it's advisable to visit with a competent local guide. Local guides can provide significant insights into the mountain's history, geology, and mythology, providing richness to the overall experience. They can also guarantee that tourists follow the principles of responsible tourism, such as staying on approved pathways and respecting vulnerable ecosystems.

Museums and Cultural Sites

The island is home to a wealth of museums and cultural attractions that provide visitors with a glimpse into Corsica's past and its distinctive character. From ancient ruins to modern art, Corsica's museums and cultural institutions give a complete experience for travelers interested in the island's rich cultural tapestry.

One of the must-visit museums in Corsica is the Museum of Corsica, located in Corte, the historical capital of Corsica. This museum presents a comprehensive overview of Corsican history and culture, from prehistoric origins to the present day. Visitors can tour exhibitions that showcase the island's geology, archaeology, anthropology, and art. The museum also exhibits a comprehensive collection of Corsican relics, including traditional clothes, utensils, and musical instruments, providing insights into the daily life and traditions of the Corsican people.

For history aficionados, a visit to the Fesch Museum in Ajaccio is a must. This museum is home to one of the most extensive collections of Italian Renaissance art outside of mainland Italy, with works by notable artists such as Botticelli, Titian, and Bellini. The museum also displays a major collection of Corsican art, including paintings, sculptures, and decorative arts that highlight the distinctive cultural heritage of the island.

Corsica is recognized for its historic ruins, and one of the most notable archaeological sites on the island is the Roman site of Aléria. Located on the eastern coast of Corsica, Aléria was once a bustling Roman colony and is now an open-air museum that provides insights into the island's Roman past. Visitors can tour the remnants of historic buildings, including a Roman forum, basilica, and thermal baths, as well as observe the objects discovered from the site, including ceramics, coins, and jewelry.

Corsica is also noted for its robust art scene. The island is home to various galleries, studios, and workshops where local artists demonstrate their talents. Visitors can experience Corsica's contemporary art scene by visiting art galleries in towns and cities such as Ajaccio, Bastia, and Porto-Vecchio, or by attending art festivals and events that promote Corsican art and culture.

Corsican Vineyards

Corsican vineyards, with their unique terroir and traditional winemaking methods, produce wines that are cherished by wine aficionados and visitors alike. In this section, we will present a thorough explanation of Corsican vineyards, including their history, grape varietals, winemaking techniques, and the experience they offer to tourists.

The history of winemaking in Corsica extends back to ancient times. The island has a long-standing winemaking culture that may be traced back to the Phoenicians, Greeks, and Romans who first grew grapes on Corsican soil. Over the years, Corsican winemaking has evolved, inspired by many cultures and winemaking techniques, resulting in a unique and distinct Corsican wine style.

One of the primary variables that contribute to the particular character of Corsican wines is the island's terroir. Corsica's diversified terroir contains a diversity of microclimates, altitudes, and soil types, which create perfect conditions for cultivating a variety of grape varieties. The island's vineyards are often positioned on slopes or terraces, taking advantage of the copious sunlight and mild sea breezes that mitigate the Mediterranean climate. This unusual combination of variables provides a distinct flavor characteristic to Corsican wines, distinguished by freshness, minerality, and complexity.

Corsican vineyards are largely planted with native grape varietals, which are well adapted to the island's soil. Some of the most important red grape varieties planted in Corsica include Niellucciu, Sciaccarellu, and Grenache, while Vermentino and Biancu Gentile are renowned white grape kinds. These indigenous grape types contribute to the particular character of Corsican wines, with their complex flavors and aromas.

One significant characteristic of Corsican winemaking is the utilization of traditional and sustainable winemaking processes. Many Corsican vineyards practice organic or biodynamic agricultural methods, avoiding the use of chemicals and pesticides in the vines. Winemakers in Corsica also typically apply traditional winemaking techniques, such as maceration carbonique, which includes fermenting whole grape clusters, and maturing wines in big oak casks, which adds richness and depth to the wines.

Visiting Corsican vineyards offers a unique experience for travelers. The island's wineries are often family-owned and operated, giving an intimate and unique experience for tourists. Many Corsican wineries provide guided tours and tastings, allowing tourists to learn about the winemaking process, try different wines, and appreciate the devotion and skill of Corsican winemakers. Some wineries also provide wine and food pairing experiences, exhibiting the gastronomic delights of Corsican cuisine, which is noted for its distinctive blend of French and Italian influences.

Tourists visiting Corsican vineyards can also appreciate the breathtaking scenery and natural beauty of the island. Corsica's vineyards are generally placed in picturesque areas, with panoramic views of the Mediterranean Sea and the island's craggy mountains. Some vineyards also provide outdoor activities, like hiking or cycling, allowing travelers to discover the magnificent wine landscapes and immerse themselves in the island's natural splendor.

Furthermore, Corsican vineyards are frequently firmly embedded in the local culture and history, giving travelers an opportunity to learn about the island's legacy. Many wineries in Corsica are housed in antique houses, some of which have been passed down through generations of winemaking families. These vineyards typically have great stories to relate to, reflecting the island's rich cultural heritage and winemaking traditions.

Top Cuisine to Try Out

As a famous tourist destination, Corsica provides a wealth of unique and tasty meals that are a must-try for every culinary fan. From rustic mountain delights to fresh marine dishes, Corsica has plenty to tickle every taste bud.

Fiadone

Fiadone is a traditional Corsican delicacy that occupies a special place in the hearts of locals and tourists alike, this delightful treat is a must-try for anybody visiting the lovely island of Corsica.

Fiadone is a sort of cheesecake created with simple yet authentic ingredients that are widely available on the island. The essential components of Fiadone are fresh brocciu cheese, eggs, sugar, lemon zest, and sometimes a splash of eau de vie, a local liqueur. The brocciu cheese used in Fiadone is a unique Corsican cheese created from the whey of sheep's milk, giving it a particularly tangy and creamy flavor.

The creation of Fiadone starts with blending the brocciu cheese with sugar, eggs, and lemon zest. The mixture is then placed into a buttered pie crust and cooked to perfection until it is golden brown and slightly firm to the touch. The outcome is a rich and creamy dessert with a beautiful balance of sweetness and tanginess that is sure to excite the taste senses.

Fiadone is primarily savored during festive occasions and celebrations, such as Easter and Christmas, but it can be purchased in pastry shops and restaurants around Corsica year-round. It is frequently served chilled, letting the ingredients mingle together and generate a rich and delicious taste. Some varieties of Fiadone additionally incorporate other ingredients such as raisins, chestnut flour, or honey, bringing a distinctive twist to the basic dish.

Apart from its great taste, Fiadone also retains cultural significance in Corsican cuisine. It is regarded as an emblem of Corsican culinary heritage, embodying the island's rich history and traditions. The use of brocciu cheese, which is created from local sheep's milk, emphasizes Corsica's agricultural traditions and closeness to its natural resources. Fiadone also reflects the warm hospitality and generosity of Corsican culture, as it is typically shared with family and friends during gatherings and celebrations.

For tourists, trying Fiadone in Corsica is not just about indulging in a delectable dessert, but also about experiencing the island's distinct culinary heritage and cultural traditions. It provides a look into the rich history, flavors, and rituals of Corsican cuisine, making it a must-try delicacy for every food enthusiast visiting the island.

Civet de Sanglier

Civet de Sanglier is a slow-cooked stew made with wild boar meat, which is abundant in the Corsican woods. The meal is normally prepared by marinating the meat in red wine, vinegar, and a variety of aromatic herbs and spices, such as juniper berries, rosemary, thyme, and bay leaves. This marinade helps to tenderize the tough wild boar meat and imbue it with rich tastes.

Once the meat has been marinated, it is next seared in a hot skillet to lock in the flavors and form a thick, caramelized crust. The beef is then cooked in the marinade together with vegetables such as carrots, onions, and celery, which add to the rich taste of the stew. The slow cooking technique helps the meat to become supple and luscious while allowing the flavors to mingle together.

One of the unique aspects of Civet de Sanglier is the use of local Corsican wine in the marinade and the stew itself. Corsica is noted for its exceptional wine production, with local grape varietals such as Nielluccio and Sciaccarello being utilized in many traditional meals. The wine gives a particular depth and complexity to the stew, making it a true expression of Corsican flavors and terroir.

Civet de Sanglier is generally served with polenta, which is a staple in Corsican cuisine. Polenta is a creamy cornmeal dish that pairs nicely with the thick and delicious stew, offering a satisfying and hearty supper. The combination of soft wild boar meat, savory marinade, and creamy polenta creates a harmonic blend of textures and flavors that is sure to thrill the senses.

Civet de Sanglier also bears cultural significance in Corsica. It is commonly served during festive occasions, including as family reunions and traditional festivities, where it draws people together to share a communal meal and celebrate Corsican culinary traditions.

Brocciu

Brocciu, a classic Corsican cheese. This distinctive cheese is profoundly rooted in Corsican culture, with its history extending back generations, and it continues to be a valued culinary gem on the island.

Brocciu is a fresh cheese prepared from sheep or goat's milk, however, a combination of both kinds of milk is also regularly used. It is often manufactured in small batches by local farmers and artisanal cheese makers, utilizing traditional methods passed down through generations. The milk is heated and curdled with the help of lemon juice or other natural acids, resulting in a soft, crumbly texture.

One of the characteristic aspects of Brocciu is its delicate flavor profile, which is a perfect blend of sweet and acidic elements. The cheese has a creamy, somewhat salty flavor with overtones of wild herbs and grass, reflecting the Corsican terroir where the sheep and goats graze on the island's beautiful pastures. The flavor of Brocciu is at its greatest during the spring months when the animals feast on fresh, aromatic foliage, making it a seasonal delicacy eagerly awaited by locals and visitors alike.

Brocciu is also strongly ingrained in Corsican culinary traditions, and it is used in a wide range of recipes. It can be served on its own, spread on toast or crackers, or included in numerous recipes, such as omelets, spaghetti, soups, and desserts. It is a versatile ingredient that gives a characteristic creaminess and tanginess to recipes, raising them to new heights.

Beyond its culinary appeal, Brocciu also retains cultural significance in Corsica. It is commonly utilized in local events and celebrations, like Easter and Christmas, where it takes center stage on the typical Corsican table. It is also utilized as a symbol of Corsican identity, signifying the island's rich agricultural tradition and the relationship between its people and the soil.

For travelers visiting Corsica, Brocciu offers a unique gastronomic experience that allows them to taste the island's flavors and customs. They may experience this wonderful cheese at local markets, specialized food shops, and restaurants throughout Corsica, where it is typically featured on menus as a highlight of Corsican cuisine. Some cheese makers also offer tours and tastings, providing an opportunity for tourists to learn about the cheese-making process and the cultural significance of Brocciu.

Figatellu

This delightful sausage, prepared from swine liver and other ingredients, maintains a special place in Corsican cuisine and culture, offering travelers a unique gourmet experience.

The manufacturing of Figatellu is an age-old tradition in Corsica, passed down from generation to generation. The sausage is commonly created with minced hog liver, pork flesh, and other spices, such as garlic, thyme, and pepper. The mixture is then put into natural casings and hand-tied, giving it a distinctive appearance.

Figatellu is recognized for its rich and robust flavor, with a little gamey flavor that comes from the hog liver. It is often cooked over an open flame or grilled, which lends a smoky flavor and crispy texture to the sausage. The aroma of Figatellu sizzling on the grill is delicious and brings travelers to local markets, restaurants, and festivals where it is widely found.

One of the distinctive qualities of Figatellu is its adaptability. It can be served in many ways, making it a versatile dish that appeals to different preferences. It can be served as an appetizer, a main meal, or even used as a component in other Corsican recipes, such as soups, stews, and pasta sauces. Figatellu is typically coupled with Corsican cheeses, olives, and bread, providing a wonderful combination of flavors that typifies Corsican cuisine.

It also retains cultural relevance in Corsica. It is strongly established in Corsican traditions and is commonly connected with family reunions, celebrations, and special occasions. Many Corsican families have their own unique recipes for Figatellu, passed down through generations, lending a feeling of pride and legacy to this iconic sausage.

For travelers visiting Corsica, Figatellu offers a unique and authentic culinary experience that reflects the island's rich gastronomic past. Sampling Figatellu invites guests to revel in the flavors and traditions of Corsican cuisine, delivering a sensory voyage through the island's culinary ecosystem. It also offers an opportunity to connect with the inhabitants, learn about their traditions, and acquire insight into Corsican culture.

Salsiccia

Salsiccia, commonly known as Corsican sausage, is a traditional delicacy that is popular among locals and tourists. This distinctive sausage is a vital feature of Corsican cuisine and gives a tasty and authentic flavor that reflects the island's culinary tradition.

Corsican sausage is produced using high-quality hog flesh, often acquired from locally grown pigs that are noted for their rich and tasty meat. The flesh is frequently seasoned with a blend of fragrant herbs and spices, including garlic, thyme, rosemary, and fennel seeds, which give the sausage its particular taste and scent. The sausage is then packed into natural casings, often made from pig intestines, and is left to dry and cure for a period of time to increase its flavor.

One of the distinguishing aspects of Corsican sausage is its range of flavors and textures. It can be obtained in several types, including fresh, smoked, and dried, with each type delivering a distinct taste experience. Fresh salsiccia is juicy and tender, with a mild and delicate flavor, making it a favorite choice for grilling or frying. Smoked salsiccia, on the other hand, has a smoky and intense flavor that is obtained by smoking the sausage over wood flames, giving it a particular aroma and taste. Dried salsiccia, also known as saucisson, is often sliced thin and eaten as a snack or part of a charcuterie board and has a solid texture with a concentrated taste that develops throughout the curing process.

Salsiccia is not only noted for its exquisite taste but also for its cultural significance in Corsican cuisine. It has a lengthy history on the island, with recipes and techniques passed down through generations of Corsican families. It is widely used in traditional Corsican meals, such as soups, stews, and pasta sauces, providing depth and richness to the flavors. It is also a fundamental ingredient in many Corsican festivals and celebrations, where it is commonly grilled or roasted over open flames, providing a joyous and communal touch to the dining experience.

For travelers visiting Corsica, trying salsiccia is a must to really immerse in the local gastronomic culture. It may be obtained in local markets, butcher shops, and restaurants throughout the island, and is commonly enjoyed as part of a leisurely lunch with family and friends. Some food enthusiasts even go on guided excursions to learn about the traditional method of manufacturing salsiccia and to try different variations from local producers.

Aubergine à la Bonifacienne

Aubergine à la Bonifacienne, also known as Bonifacio-style eggplant, Corsica is known for its rich culinary tradition, which is greatly influenced by French and Italian cuisines, and Aubergine à la Bonifacienne is a delicious example of this fusion.

The dish normally consists of roasted or fried eggplant slices that are stacked with a savory tomato and meat sauce, and often topped with melted cheese. The word "Bonifacienne" relates to the town of Bonifacio, located on the southern tip of Corsica, which is noted for its scenic cliffs and medieval old town. Aubergine à la Bonifacienne is a renowned traditional meal in this region, cherished for its rustic, robust flavors and easy yet fulfilling preparation.

To create Aubergine à la Bonifacienne, thick slices of eggplant are traditionally salted and allowed to settle for a brief time to drain out any extra moisture and bitterness. The eggplant slices are then cleaned and dried before being roasted or fried until they are brown and tender. Meanwhile, a savory tomato and meat sauce is cooked, often using ground beef or pig, as well as garlic, onions, and herbs such as thyme and rosemary. The sauce is cooked until it thickens and produces a rich, powerful flavor.

Once the eggplant slices and meat sauce are ready, they are placed in a baking dish, with the eggplant providing the base, followed by the meat sauce, and often topped with grated cheese, such as Parmesan or mozzarella. The dish is then roasted in the oven until it is bubbling and brown on top. The result is a delectable, aromatic dish with layers of soft eggplant, savory meat sauce, and melted cheese, all coming together in a beautiful blend of flavors.

It is often served as a main meal, accompanied by a simple salad or crusty bread to soak up the delectable sauce. It is a dish that is great for showing the natural tastes of Corsican ingredients, with the eggplant taking center stage and the meat sauce providing depth and richness. The combination of roasted or fried eggplant, acidic tomato sauce, and melting cheese makes a soothing and fulfilling dish that is sure to please any food enthusiast.

Soupe Corse

Soupe Corse, also known as Corsican Soup, this rustic soup is a beloved culinary jewel that shows the rich tastes of Corsican cuisine, known for its simple yet wonderful ingredients.

The base of Soupe Corse is often created with a combination of legumes, including white beans, lentils, and chickpeas, which are cooked in a flavorful broth made from beef or hog bones. The soup is then infused with fragrant herbs and spices, such as rosemary, thyme, and bay leaves, which lend depth and richness to the meal.

One of the major ingredients that make Soupe Corse special is the use of indigenous Corsican charcuterie, which is a form of preserved meat. Corsica is famed for its high-quality charcuterie, which includes specialties like lonzu (cured pig loin), coppa (cured pork shoulder), and figatellu (cured pork liver sausage). These tasty meats are often cut and added to the soup, infusing it with their particular smoky and salty aromas.

Soupe Corse often incorporates other components that are widely found in Corsican cuisines, such as vegetables like carrots, onions, and leeks, as well as pasta or rice, which provide heartiness to the dish. The soup is often heated gently, enabling the flavors to mingle together and create a powerful and soothing bowl of delight.

Soupe Corse is not only a wonderful and satisfying food, but it also bears cultural significance for Corsicans. It is commonly served as a family supper or a communal dish, bringing people together around the table to share in its warmth and flavor. It is also a symbol of Corsican hospitality, as it is typically offered to guests as a sign of welcome and generosity.

As with many traditional recipes, there are regional versions of Soupe Corse that differ from town to village or family to family, with each cook adding their own particular touch. Some may like a thicker soup with more beans and charcuterie, while others may prefer a lighter version with more veggies. Nevertheless, the core of Soupe Corse remains the same - a substantial and flavorsome soup that symbolizes the culinary legacy of Corsica.

Grilled Seafood

Corsica's geographic location makes it a wonderful site for seafood enthusiasts. The island is surrounded by the brilliant blue seas of the Mediterranean Sea, which are teeming with a rich assortment of fish and shellfish. Local fishermen haul in their catch of the day, and many restaurants in Corsica offer an outstanding assortment of freshly caught seafood.

One of the most popular ways to prepare seafood in Corsica is grilling. Grilling is a traditional cooking method in Corsican cuisine, where the fish is cooked over an open flame, frequently utilizing local wood or herbs to create a particular smokey flavor. The simplicity of grilling allows the natural tastes of the seafood to come through, resulting in a wonderful and authentic culinary experience.

The sorts of seafood that are regularly grilled in Corsica vary depending on the season and availability, but some of the more popular selections include fish such as sea bream, sea bass, and mullet, as well as shellfish like squid, octopus, and prawns. These fresh ingredients are commonly marinated in a blend of olive oil, lemon juice, garlic, and local herbs, which improves their flavors and adds a touch of Mediterranean brightness.

Grilled fish in Corsica is often served with modest accompaniments that enhance the natural flavors of the seafood. These may contain grilled veggies like zucchini, eggplant, and peppers, as well as local cheeses, such as brocciu, a fresh Corsican cheese made from ewe's milk. Rustic bread or polenta are also typically served alongside grilled seafood, soaking up the delectable juices and giving a hearty flavor to the dish.

In addition to the delectable flavors, the pleasure of having grilled seafood in Corsica is also about the environment. Many restaurants in Corsica offer outside dining with magnificent views of the sea, allowing diners to relish their meal while taking in the breathtaking surroundings. The laid-back and easygoing ambiance, along with the warm Mediterranean air, contributes to the overall enjoyment of the eating experience.

Falculelle

Falculelle is a sort of Corsican pancake that is produced with basic, yet delicious ingredients. The basic components of this recipe are chestnut flour, water, olive oil, and salt. The batter is stirred until it reaches a smooth consistency and is then put onto a heated griddle or cast-iron skillet, making little pancakes with a unique round shape. The pancakes are baked until they create a crispy crust on the exterior while remaining soft and slightly chewy on the inside.

The use of chestnut flour in Falculelle is significant, as it shows Corsica's rich agricultural background. Chestnuts have been a main crop in Corsica for ages, and their flour is utilized in many traditional cuisines. The nutty flavor of chestnut flour provides a particular depth of taste to the Falculelle, giving it a genuinely authentic Corsican meal.

It is also noted for its cultural significance. It is typically prepared for festive occasions and celebrations in Corsica, such as weddings, harvest festivals, and religious gatherings. Sharing Falculelle with family and friends is a valued custom that brings people together and honors Corsican culinary heritage.

Falculelle is often served as a snack or an appetizer, and it can be savored on its own or coupled with other Corsican specialties. It is generally served hot, fresh from the griddle, and can be eaten with your fingers or a spoon. Some locals also prefer spreading honey or olive oil over the pancakes for an added burst of flavor.

For tourists, trying Falculelle is an opportunity to immerse oneself in Corsican culture and culinary traditions. From seeing the experienced local cooks prepare the batter and cook the pancakes, to relishing the unique flavors and textures, every bite of Falculelle is a sensory delight. The dish gives a whole experience, delivering an insight into the history, culture, and culinary legacy of Corsica.

Cannelloni

This culinary delicacy is a sort of pasta dish that comprises cannelloni tubes stuffed with a savory filling, generally made with meat and cheese, and baked in a rich tomato sauce. Let's take a closer look at this delectable dish and its components.

The pasta used in Cannelloni Corse is cannelloni tubes, which are big cylindrical pasta tubes prepared from wheat flour and water. The tubes are normally boiled until they are al dente, or firm to the bite, before being filled with the delightful filling. The filling is the heart of Cannelloni Corse and is what sets it apart from other pasta meals.

The filling for Cannelloni Corse often consists of a combination of meat and cheese. Common meats used in the filling include ground beef, pork, or a combination of both. The meat is often cooked with aromatic herbs like thyme, rosemary, and garlic to infuse it with exquisite flavors. Cheese, such as ricotta or Parmesan, is then combined with cooked meat to add creaminess and enhance the overall flavor.

Once the filling is made, it is gently spooned into the cooked cannelloni tubes, which are then coiled up to produce compact cylinders. The filled tubes are then placed in a baking dish, nestled in a bed of rich tomato sauce, which is produced from tomatoes, onions, and other ingredients. The meal is then roasted in the oven until the pasta is cooked through and the flavors have melted together, creating a delectable and aromatic dish.

Cannelloni Corse is normally eaten hot, right from the oven, and is often garnished with a sprinkle of freshly grated Parmesan cheese and chopped fresh basil for extra flavor and freshness. The combination of soft pasta, delicious meat and cheese filling, and acidic tomato sauce creates a symphony of flavors that are both comfortable and gratifying.

This dish is not only excellent but also a reflection of Corsican cuisine and culture. Corsican cuisine is noted for its rustic and hearty flavors, influenced by the island's topography and history. The use of simple, fresh ingredients and traditional cooking techniques are hallmarks of Corsican cuisine, and Cannelloni Corse is a superb illustration of this culinary history.

Patrimonio Wine

One of the hidden gems of Corsican gastronomy is the world-renowned Patrimonio wine, which occupies a particular place in the hearts of wine connoisseurs and travelers alike.

Patrimonio wine is made in the wine-growing region of Patrimonio, located in the northern portion of Corsica, France. The location, famed for its rocky cliffs, excellent soil, and Mediterranean climate, provides an ideal environment for grape growth. The vineyards in Patrimonio are set amidst scenic scenery, including terraced slopes, ancient villages, and spectacular sea vistas, making it a prominent destination for wine tourism.

The history of winemaking in Patrimonio extends back to the Roman Empire, and the region has a long-standing reputation for producing high-quality wines. However, it was only in 1968 that Patrimonio was recognized as an official appellation d'origine contrôlée (AOC), which reflects its protected designation of origin status. Today, Patrimonio wine is widely respected for its particular features, representing the terroir of the region.

The major grape variety utilized in Patrimonio wine production is Niellucciu, which is indigenous to Corsica and is often compared to the Sangiovese grape. Niellucciu lends the aromas of red fruits, spices, and herbs to the wine, giving it a distinct Corsican personality. Other grape varieties such as Vermentino (white) and Muscat à Petits Grains (Muscat Blanc) are also used in the creation of Patrimonio wine, adding to its richness and complexity.

Patrimonio wine is typically dry and full-bodied, with a rich and strong flavor character. The red wines are characterized by their dark ruby hue, with aromas of red and black fruits, Mediterranean herbs, and a hint of minerality. The white wines are crisp and fragrant, showcasing the aromas of citrus, white flowers, and exotic fruits. Rosé wines, created from Niellucciu grapes, are especially popular in Patrimonio, delivering a pleasant and fruity taste.

Patrimonio wine is strongly connected with Corsican culture and history. Many wineries in Patrimonio are tiny, family-owned properties that have been passed down through generations, and their winemaking processes are profoundly anchored in tradition. Wine festivals and events are an intrinsic part of the local culture, with festivities and tastings taking place throughout the year, allowing visitors a unique glimpse into Corsican wine tradition.

For wine connoisseurs and tourists alike, a visit to Patrimonio is a must. The region has various wine estates and cellars that are open for tastings and tours, allowing an opportunity to learn about the winemaking process, meet enthusiastic winemakers, and enjoy the tastes of Patrimonio wine. The scenic vineyards and stunning landscapes give a breathtaking backdrop for wine tasting, making it a really unforgettable experience.

Best Time To Visit

When arranging a trip to Corsica, timing is key to ensure you get the most out of your visit. So, when is the ideal time to visit Corsica.

Corsica experiences a Mediterranean climate with warm, dry summers and mild, wet winters. The main tourist season in Corsica is during the summer months of June to August when the weather is nice and the island is packed with activities. However, the perfect time to visit Corsica depends on your choices and interests.

Summer (June to August)
Summer is the busiest time to visit Corsica, with mild temperatures ranging from 25 to 30 degrees Celsius, making it excellent for beach activities, water sports, and outdoor adventures. The sea is at its warmest during this period, great for swimming and snorkeling. The island comes alive with festivals, parties, and energetic nightlife, making it an excellent time for individuals who prefer a lively atmosphere.

However, the high season also means crowded beaches, greater rates for lodgings, and lengthier lineups at popular sites. If you prefer a more leisurely and quieter experience, summer may not be the greatest time to visit Corsica.

Spring (April to May) and Autumn (September to October)
Spring and autumn are considered the shoulder seasons in Corsica, bringing good weather with fewer crowds compared to the high summer months. During spring, the island blossoms with brilliant flowers and the countryside comes

alive with vegetation, making it great for nature lovers and hikers.

Autumn, on the other hand, brings pleasant weather and is a good time to visit Corsica for wine connoisseurs, as it is the grape harvesting season. You can also enjoy the gorgeous fall foliage and experience Corsican culture at local events at this time.

Both spring and autumn offer a more calm and serene experience, with lower lodging fees and fewer crowded attractions, making it a perfect time to visit if you prefer a more casual and laid-back vacation.

Winter (November to March)
Winter is the low season in Corsica, with colder temperatures ranging from 10 to 15 degrees Celsius, with occasional rains. However, it might still be a terrific time to visit if you prefer outdoor activities such as hiking, skiing, or seeing Corsica's charming villages.

Corsica's mountains are covered with snow during winter, allowing chances for skiing and snowboarding at resorts like Val d'Ese and Ghisoni-Capannelle. The island's landscape also transforms into a winter wonderland, affording spectacular views of snow-capped hills and frozen lakes.

Winter is a wonderful time to discover Corsica's distinct culture and traditions, as the island holds different winter festivals and events, including Christmas markets and local celebrations.

The best time to visit Corsica depends on your choices and interests. Summer is perfect for beach lovers and people who want a bustling atmosphere, while spring and autumn provide pleasant weather, fewer crowds, and lower pricing. Winter is great for outdoor enthusiasts and anyone interested in seeing Corsican culture during the low season. Consider your favorite activities, budget, and the degree of crowd you are comfortable with when arranging your trip to Corsica.

Traveling Itinerary

With its magnificent beaches, steep mountains, rich history, and unique culture, Corsica offers a broad selection of activities and attractions that may be experienced in both one and two-week itineraries. Whether you prefer relaxing on the beach, outdoor adventures, or cultural encounters, Corsica has something for you. In this complete guide, we will present full itineraries for both one and two weeks of vacation in Corsica, including recommendations for accommodations, activities, and must-see sights.

1 Week Itinerary for Corsica

Day 1-2: Ajaccio - Arrival and City Exploration
Start your Corsican experience by flying into Ajaccio, the capital city of Corsica. Ajaccio is famed for its historical significance as the birthplace of Napoleon Bonaparte, and you may begin your journey by exploring the city's attractions associated with the famous French military leader. Visit the Maison Bonaparte, which is now a museum dedicated to Napoleon's life, and the Cathédrale Notre-Dame-de-l'Assomption where he was baptized. Stroll down the tiny streets of the old town, known as the Vieille Ville, and indulge in some local food at one of the many eateries.

Day 3-4: Calvi - Beaches and Citadel
On day 3, head to Calvi, a lovely town on the northwest coast of Corsica. Calvi is noted for its lovely sandy beaches and its well-preserved fortress, which offers panoramic views of the town and the surrounding coastline. Spend your days soaking in the sun on Calvi's beaches, or take a boat ride to explore the adjacent Calanques de Piana, a UNESCO World Heritage

Site noted for its spectacular red granite cliffs and crystal-clear waters.

Day 5-6: Porto-Vecchio - Beaches and Nightlife
On day 5, make your way to the southeast coast of Corsica to Porto-Vecchio, noted for its white sandy beaches, such as Palombaggia and Santa Giulia, which are among the most beautiful beaches in Corsica. Relax on the beaches, go swimming or snorkeling in the turquoise waters, or enjoy water sports activities such as paddleboarding or kayaking. In the evenings, come to the town center for a vibrant nightlife scene, with several bars, restaurants, and clubs to select from.

Day 7: Bonifacio - Cliffs and Medieval Town
On the last day of your one-week journey, explore Bonifacio's spectacular cliffs overlooking the sea and its well-preserved medieval village. Take a boat tour to explore the limestone cliffs and caves, or walk along the attractive alleys of the old town, known as the Haute Ville, and visit the ancient landmarks such as the Citadel and the Church of Sainte Marie Majeure. Don't miss the chance to indulge in some local seafood at one of Bonifacio's seafood restaurants.

2 Week Itinerary for Corsica

For those with more time to explore Corsica, a two-week plan provides for a more in-depth tour of the island, including some off-the-beaten-path sites.

Days 1-4: Ajaccio and Surroundings
Follow the same itinerary as the one-week plan for Ajaccio and local sights, but spend some additional time visiting the surroundings. Visit the adjacent Îles Sanguinaires, a series of

rugged islands famed for their red granite cliffs and stunning sunsets. You can take a boat tour or trek along the coastal trails to appreciate the gorgeous views and spot local species such as seabirds and seals. You can also visit the Parc Naturel Régional de Corse, a protected natural park that spans a considerable piece of Corsica's interior, affording chances for hiking, bird watching, and experiencing Corsica's rich flora and fauna.

Days 5-7: Corte - Mountain Adventures and Corsican Culture

Head to Corte, explore the Citadel, an ancient fortification that gives panoramic views of the surrounding mountains, and visit the Musée de la Corse, a museum dedicated to Corsican culture and history. Take a hike in the adjacent Restonica Valley, noted for its spectacular granite cliffs, crystal-clear rivers, and picturesque mountain villages. You can go hiking, rock climbing, or swimming in the refreshing alpine streams.

Days 8-10: Bastia and Cap Corse - Coastal Charm and Scenic Drives

Drive to Bastia, located on the northeastern coast of Corsica, and discover this dynamic port city noted for its antique buildings, lively markets, and colorful streets. Visit the 16th-century Saint-Nicolas Church, the Oratoire de l'Immaculée Conception, and the Old Port with its busy ambiance. Take a leisurely stroll along the shoreline and eat the local food at one of the many restaurants.

From Bastia, you may also enjoy a scenic drive along the gorgeous Cap Corse, the short peninsula that reaches into the Mediterranean Sea. Explore the picturesque fishing communities, such as Erbalunga and Nonza, noted for their unique architecture and stunning coastal vistas. Visit the

Mattei Cap Corse Distillery, noted for its iconic Corsican liqueurs, and enjoy the panoramic scenery from the numerous locations along the road.

Days 11-14: Propriano and Sartène - Beaches, Wine Tasting, and Cultural Heritage

Drive to the southwest coast of Corsica and spend your last days at Propriano, a renowned seaside resort town famed for its gorgeous beaches and blue waters. Relax on the beaches, go snorkeling or scuba diving to explore the underwater world, or take a boat journey to surrounding islands such as Îles Lavezzi. In the evenings, savor the local cuisine at the seaside restaurants, noted for their fresh seafood and Corsican specialties.

From Propriano, you may also explore Sartène, a magnificent hilltop town famed for its rich cultural legacy and Corsican traditions. Wander through the small alleyways lined with ancient stone buildings, visit the Church of Santa Maria Assunta, and explore the ancient megalithic structures dispersed around the region. Don't miss the opportunity to taste the local wines, as Sartène is recognized for its vineyards and wine production.

On your last day, you can relax on the beaches of Propriano or take a boat ride to explore the adjacent Gulf of Valinco, noted for its breathtaking splendor and crystal-clear waters. Alternatively, you can take a leisurely drive down the coastal roads, stopping at lovely villages and magnificent overlooks, before traveling back to Ajaccio for your departure.

Visiting On a Budget

Visiting Corsica on a budget can be an interesting and memorable experience for tourists who are eager to explore this lovely Mediterranean island without breaking the bank. While Corsica can be expensive, with proper preparation and budgeting, it is possible to enjoy a terrific holiday without splurging.

Accommodation is one of the biggest expenses for travelers, although there are budget-friendly options in Corsica. One option is to stay in budget hotels or hostels, especially in smaller towns or off-the-beaten-path places. These motels can offer low rates and provide basic amenities for a comfortable stay. Another budget-friendly alternative is camping. Corsica has various campgrounds that are inexpensive and provide possibilities to appreciate the island's natural beauty. Camping also allows people to cook their meals, which can save on eating charges.

Transportation is another factor to consider while visiting Corsica on a budget. Renting a car can be costly, so choosing public transportation can be more budget-friendly. Corsica offers a solid bus system that connects major towns and villages, allowing people to explore the island without the need for a car. Additionally, using local trains or ferries to travel between different sections of Corsica can be a more cheap choice compared to hiring a car.

a meal is a significant part of the Corsican experience, and while dining out in restaurants may be expensive, there are ways to save on meal costs. One option is to visit local markets and grocery stores to buy fresh vegetables, bread, and other goods for picnics or meals made at accommodations with kitchen facilities. Trying out local street cuisine or takeout options can also be more budget-friendly than dining in restaurants. Corsica is famed for its great local cuisine, so be sure to taste the local delicacies, such as charcuterie, cheese, and fish, which can be purchased at more moderate costs in local markets.

Exploring Corsica's natural splendor is a must, and there are budget-friendly ways to do so. Many of Corsica's biggest attractions, such as its beautiful beaches, attractive villages, and stunning hiking routes, are free or low-cost. Taking use of the island's natural beauty by hiking, swimming, or simply relaxing on the beach can be a budget-friendly way to explore Corsica. Additionally, visiting Corsica during the shoulder season (April to June or September to November) might assist save on expenditures, as accommodation and transportation charges tend to be lower compared to the busy summer season.

When it comes to touring and attractions, it's crucial to prioritize and prepare ahead to get the most out of your cash. Corsica has various historic monuments, museums, and cultural institutions that may charge access fees. Researching and choosing the must-visit sites can help travelers avoid unnecessary spending and choose the ones that best fit their interests and budget.

Finally, it's necessary to be conscious of other expenses such as souvenirs, entertainment, and miscellaneous fees. Setting a daily budget and tracking expenses can help travelers remain within their budget and prevent overspending. Avoiding unnecessary expenses and being careful with discretionary spending might help stretch your budget and make your trip to Corsica more reasonable.

Opting for budget-friendly lodging, using public transportation, discovering local markets, enjoying outdoor activities, and being cautious of expenses can help travelers make the most of their budget and create an amazing experience on this lovely Mediterranean island.

Getting Around

Getting about Corsica, albeit not without its hurdles, is rather easy and rewarding. This section will provide a thorough explanation of how to move around Corsica, including the best types of transportation, the routes to take, and advice for a comfortable voyage.

By Car

One of the greatest ways to discover Corsica is by renting a car. With a car, you may have the flexibility to explore the island at your own leisure, travel picturesque routes, and visit rural settlements that are otherwise impossible to access. There are various car rental firms in Corsica, and you can rent a car at the airport, in the cities, or online. However, keep in mind that the roads in Corsica are often narrow, twisting, and steep, so driving might be tough. It's vital to be cautious and respect the traffic rules, especially whether driving in the mountains or along the shore.

By Bus

Another alternative for getting around Corsica is by taking the bus. The bus network in Corsica is substantial, serving most major towns and cities. The buses are comfortable, air-conditioned, and quite affordable. However, the bus schedules can be irregular, and certain lines are only available during the high season. Therefore, it's vital to verify the bus timetable before arranging your journey. One of the nicest bus routes is the Train des Pignes, which travels from Ajaccio to Corte and offers spectacular views of the countryside.

By Train

The Train de la Balagne is a picturesque train line that goes from Calvi to L'Île-Rousse. The train journey is a terrific chance to observe the magnificent Corsican landscape, with its olive trees, vineyards, and seaside scenery. The trains are comfortable, air-conditioned, and very affordable, but they might be busy during the high season. It's recommended to purchase your tickets in advance, especially if you're traveling during the peak tourist season.

By Ferry

If you're traveling to Corsica from mainland France or Italy, the best way to get there is by ferry. Corsica is well connected by ferry to various ports in France and Italy, notably Marseille, Nice, Toulon, Livorno, and Genoa. There are various ferry companies operating on the island, and you can order your tickets online or at the ports. However, bear in mind that the boat timings can be irregular, especially during the high season, so it's crucial to verify the itinerary before organizing your trip.

By Plane

If you're short on time, you may fly to Corsica from several major cities in Europe. Corsica has four airports, located in Ajaccio, Bastia, Calvi, and Figari. Several airlines operate flights to Corsica, including Air Corsica, EasyJet, Ryanair, and Volotea. However, flying can be pricey, and you may lose out on the gorgeous beauty that Corsica has to offer.

Tips for a Smooth Journey

- Plan your route in advance and examine the timings of the numerous forms of transportation.

- Rent a car if you want to explore Corsica at your own pace.

- Be cautious when driving on tiny and twisty roads.

- Book your rail tickets in advance, especially during the high season.

- Check the boat schedules before arranging your journey, and book your tickets in advance if feasible.

- Pack light if you're traveling the bus or rail, as luggage storage can be restricted.

- Bring a map or GPS gadget to help you traverse the island.

- Carry plenty of water and snacks, especially if you're hiking or exploring rural locations.

- Respect the local culture and environment by obeying the local norms, traditions, and legislation.

- Learn a few simple words in French, as it is the official language in Corsica.

- Be prepared for the risk of strikes or delays in public transit, as they can occur in Corsica.

- Take attention to the weather conditions, especially if you're planning to drive or walk in the mountains, as Corsica's weather can change suddenly.

- Respect the natural beauty of Corsica by practicing responsible tourism, such as avoiding trash, keeping on approved routes, and not disturbing wildlife.

- Keep in mind that some rural regions in Corsica may not have adequate mobile phone reception, so it's important to have a backup plan for communication.

- Stay hydrated and apply sunscreen, as Corsica can have hot and sunny weather, especially during the summer months.

Whether you choose to rent a car, ride the bus, rail, ferry, or fly, there are different options to fit your interests and budget. Planning your visit in advance, being flexible with scheduling, and respecting the local culture and environment will ensure a smooth and pleasurable trip.

Shopping for Souvenirs

Whether you are a tourist seeking a memento to remember your vacation or a gift for your loved ones back home, Corsica provides a wealth of unique and authentic souvenirs that reflect the soul of this fascinating island. In this section, we will examine the rich tradition of souvenir buying in Corsica, emphasizing some of the must-buy goods and the best venues to purchase them.

Corsican souvenirs are not just conventional trinkets; they are often handcrafted by local artists utilizing traditional methods and materials, making them really special and symbolic of the island's rich cultural heritage. One of the most recognizable souvenirs from Corsica is the Corsican knife, known as the "curnicciulu" or "curniciellu" in the Corsican language. This classic folding knife is not only a functional tool for everyday use, but it also bears significant cultural value as a symbol of Corsican identity and pride. The blade of the Corsican knife is normally made of high-quality stainless steel, while the handle is carved from a variety of materials, including wood, bone, or horn, often embellished with complex carvings or inlays. The Corsican knife comes in numerous sizes and styles, from the compact and functional "Vendetta" knife to the more intricate and artistic "Pied-du-Corsu" knife, making it a flexible and significant keepsake for any traveler.

Another favorite Corsican gift is the "cédrat," or citron, which is a variety of lemon-like fruit endemic to the island. Corsican cédrat is highly appreciated for its peculiar aroma and flavor, and it is used in a number of culinary and cosmetic goods, including liqueurs, soaps, and perfumes. One of the most famous cédrat-based products is the "Eau de Cédrat," a pleasant and energizing citrus fragrance that reflects the spirit of Corsica's Mediterranean setting. You may get cédrat-based items in many local shops and markets throughout Corsica, especially in the towns of Calvi and Bonifacio, where cédrat is cultivated and harvested.

Corsican honey is another must-buy keepsake for culinary lovers and experts. Corsica's pristine natural environment, with its rich flora and mild climate, provides the ideal circumstances for honey production, resulting in high-quality, aromatic honey with distinctive aromas. The island is noted for its "maquis" honey, which is generated from the nectar of the wildflowers that blanket the Corsican countryside. Corsican honey comes in numerous flavors, including chestnut, heather, and maquis, and it is often sold in attractive small jars covered with rustic labels, making it a delightful and authentic souvenir to bring back home.

For wine connoisseurs, Corsican wine is a must-try and a wonderful keepsake to take home. Corsica has a long and rich winemaking culture, reaching back to ancient times, and it is noted for its distinctive and high-quality wines. The island's distinctive terroir, with its different microclimates and soils, yields a wide range of grape types, including Nielluccio, Vermentino, and Sciaccarellu, which are used to make red, white, and rosé wines. Corsican wines are generally defined by their freshness, complexity, and unique flavors, and they mix nicely with Corsica's delicious local cuisine. You can get Corsican wines in many local shops and wineries, and some of the best-known wine districts in Corsica include Patrimonio, Ajaccio, and Figari.

Corsica is also recognized for its brilliant and colorful handicrafts, which make for unique and beautiful souvenirs.

One of the most famous handicrafts from Corsica is the "tapis corse," or Corsican rug, which is weaved using ancient techniques passed down through generations. Corsican rugs are noted for their detailed designs, brilliant colors, and durability, and they often feature Corsica's natural landscapes, traditional symbols, or historical motifs. These wonderful rugs are not only useful but also a piece of art that lends a touch of Corsican culture to any home. You may buy Corsican rugs in specialist shops and marketplaces throughout the island, especially in the towns of Corte and Bastia.

Corsica is also recognized for its unique and magnificent jewelry, which makes for a memorable and cherished souvenir. Corsican jewelry commonly contains symbols and motifs that reflect the island's history, culture, and natural beauty. One famous symbol is the "muvra," which is a mythological Corsican animal resembling a wild boar. The muvra is thought to be a guardian and protector of Corsica, and it is typically represented in jewelry as a necklace, broach, or bracelet. Corsican jewelry is often handcrafted utilizing traditional methods and materials, such as silver, coral, or semi-precious stones, and it highlights the expertise and artistry of local jewelers. You can discover Corsican jewelry in specialist shops and boutiques throughout the island, and it makes for a memorable and lasting keepsake to cherish for years to come.

When it comes to shopping for souvenirs in Corsica, one of the greatest places to visit is the local markets, which are a dynamic and busy hub of local life and culture. One of the most famous markets in Corsica is the "Marché de l'Abbatucci" in Ajaccio, which is held every morning except Mondays and provides a wide selection of local items, including Corsican charcuterie, cheeses, wines, honey, and handicrafts. Another popular market is the "Marché de Bastia" in Bastia, which is famed for its fresh food, fish, and local delights, as well as its handicrafts and souvenirs. These markets are not only a terrific place to purchase authentic Corsican products but also an opportunity to mingle with locals, learn about Corsica's history and traditions, and immerse yourself in the island's vibrant atmosphere.

Corsica is also home to many specialty shops and boutiques that offer a wide choice of souvenirs and local items. The villages of Calvi and Bonifacio, in particular, are recognized for their quaint shops that sell a range of Corsican goods, including knives, honey, wines, pottery, textiles, and jewelry. These shops generally include unusual and high-quality things that are handcrafted by local craftsmen, making them genuinely special and original souvenirs to take back home. Exploring the small streets and alleyways of Corsica's cities and villages is a pleasant experience in itself, as you can stumble upon hidden jewels and uncover the island's rich artistic and cultural legacy.

When shopping for souvenirs in Corsica, it is vital to look for products that are branded as "made in Corsica" or "produit corse," which ensures that you are getting legitimate and locally created goods. These products are frequently of superior quality and are a true reflection of Corsica's cultural character and customs. Supporting local artisans and businesses by buying real Corsican souvenirs not only allows you to bring home a piece of Corsica but also contributes to the preservation of the island's distinctive tradition and culture.

Tour Package Options

In this area, we will discuss the numerous tour package alternatives available for Corsica, providing a thorough explanation to assist travelers plan their perfect Corsican trip.

Classic Corsica Trip Package
This trip package is suitable for first-time travelers who want to discover the highlights of Corsica. It normally includes a guided tour of the island's capital, Ajaccio, which is famous for being the birthplace of Napoleon Bonaparte. The package may also include trips to other key cities like Bastia, Calvi, and Bonifacio, each with its particular charm and historical value. Additionally, the Classic Corsica Tour Package may include excursions to Corsica's natural beauties, such as the Calanques de Piana, the Scandola Nature Reserve, and the Restonica Valley.

This vacation package frequently includes hotel, transportation, and guided tours, providing a hassle-free way to see the finest of Corsica.

Adventure Corsica Tour Package
For thrill-seekers and outdoor enthusiasts, the Adventure Corsica Tour Package provides an array of fascinating activities. This package may include hiking or trekking tours to Corsica's famous GR20 track. It may also involve water sports activities such as kayaking, snorkeling, or diving in Corsica's crystal-clear waters. Additionally, the Adventure Corsica Tour Package may include options for canyoning, rock climbing, or horseback riding in Corsica's rough environment. This tour package is great for people who are wishing to add an

135

adrenaline rush to their Corsican trip and explore the island's natural beauty in an adventurous way.

Culinary Corsica Tour Package
Corsica is recognized for its exquisite food that contains a blend of French and Italian influences, combined with its unique local flavors. The Culinary Corsica Tour Package is created for foodies who wish to revel in the island's gastronomic wonders. This package may include guided food tours that take guests on a gourmet adventure to experience Corsica's traditional cuisine. It may also involve visits to local markets, wineries, and olive oil mills to learn about Corsican food production. Additionally, the Culinary Corsica Tour Package may provide cooking workshops, where guests can learn to prepare Corsican specialties from local chefs. This tour package is a fantastic alternative for individuals who wish to experience the flavors of Corsica and immerse themselves in its culinary culture.

Beach Escape Corsica Tour Package
With its gorgeous coastline and immaculate beaches, Corsica is heaven for beach lovers. The Beach Escape Corsica Tour Package is created for individuals who wish to relax, unwind, and soak up the sun on Corsica's stunning beaches. This package may include nights at premium beachside resorts or boutique hotels, with plenty of leisure time to enjoy the sandy coasts and blue waters of Corsica. It may also include extra water sports activities, such as snorkeling, paddleboarding, or boat tours to discover Corsica's hidden coves and isolated beaches. This tour package is great for people who wish to experience the ultimate beach holiday and enjoy Corsica's lovely coastal beauty.

Cultural Corsica Tour Package

Corsica has a rich cultural legacy, shaped by its past and unique culture. The Cultural Corsica Tour Package is created for people who want to delve into Corsica's intriguing culture, traditions, and history. This package may include excursions to Corsica's museums, such as the Museum of Corsican Ethnography in Corte, or the Museum of Bonaparte House in Ajaccio, which provides insights into the life and times of Napoleon Bonaparte. The package may also include guided excursions of Corsica's ancient towns and villages, such as Sartène, noted for its medieval architecture and cultural history, or Pigna, a lovely village famous for its artists and local crafts. Additionally, the Cultural Corsica Tour Package may include opportunities to visit local festivals, such as the Corsican polyphonic singing festival, or participate in cultural programs, such as studying traditional Corsican music or dance. This travel package is great for people who want to immerse themselves in Corsica's rich culture and heritage and obtain a deeper grasp of the island's unique personality.

Family Fun Corsica Tour Package
Corsica is also a terrific destination for families with kids, and the Family Fun Corsica Tour Package is created to cater to the needs and interests of families. This package may include family-friendly lodgings with facilities such as swimming pools, kids' clubs, and playgrounds. It may also include activities that are ideal for children, such as beach outings, hiking on easy routes, or exploring Corsica's natural reserves. The package may also include excursions to family-friendly sites, such as the Corsica Aventure Park, an outdoor adventure park with zip lines and treetop courses, or the Aquarium of Corsica, where youngsters can learn about the island's aquatic life. Additionally, the Family Fun Corsica Tour Package may include cultural activities that are informative and amusing for kids, such as interactive museums or seminars on Corsican

crafts. This trip package is great for families who wish to make lasting memories and have a fun-filled vacation in Corsica.

Customized Corsica Tour Package
If none of the pre-designed tour packages suit your interests or preferences, several tour operators also offer customized Corsica Tour Packages that can be adapted to your individual needs. With a bespoke trip package, you have the opportunity to set your own itinerary, accommodations, activities, and duration of stay. You can work with a tour operator to build a personalized Corsican experience that caters to your interests, whether it's a hiking, wine tasting, beach hopping, or cultural immersion. This trip package is suitable for people who desire a customized and bespoke Corsican vacation that suits their specific preferences and interests.

When choosing a trip package, it's vital to consider your interests, tastes, and budget, and engage with a reputable tour operator to ensure a well-planned and pleasurable holiday. With its magnificent landscapes, rich cultural heritage, and numerous activities, Corsica is a location worth visiting, and a well-designed tour package can help you make the most of your Corsican trip.

Tourist Safety Tips

As a major tourist location, it's crucial for guests to emphasize safety during their visit. Here are some key tourist safety precautions to guarantee a safe and pleasurable vacation to Corsica.

Be aware of the weather: Corsica experiences a Mediterranean climate with hot, dry summers and moderate, wet winters. During the summer months, temperatures can skyrocket, so it's vital to stay hydrated, use sunscreen, and seek shade when needed. In winter, the island can experience significant rainfall, so be prepared with suitable clothing and footwear to avoid slipping on wet areas.

Take measures in the water: Corsica's crystal-clear seas are a significant draw for tourists, but it's vital to practice caution when swimming or partaking in aquatic activities. Pay heed to any warning signs or flags on the beaches, as they reflect the safety conditions for swimming. It's suggested to swim in specified locations with lifeguards present and avoid problematic places with strong currents or harmful sea life.

Be careful of hiking hazards: Corsica is famed for its magnificent hiking routes, but they can pose difficulties if not tackled with prudence. Before beginning on a hike, check the weather forecast, dress in appropriate footwear and clothing, and bring adequate water and food. Stick to defined trails and avoid wandering into restricted or unknown regions. It's also important to inform someone about your trekking plans and carry a charged phone for emergencies.

Secure your belongings: As with any tourist site, it's necessary to safeguard your belongings in Corsica. Avoid leaving your belongings unsecured on the beach or in your car. Use lockers or safes offered by hotels to store your valuable belongings. Be aware of pickpockets in crowded areas, such as markets or public transport, and keep your possessions secure at all times.

Drive safely: If you plan to rent a car and tour Corsica by road, prioritize safe driving practices. Corsica's steep landscape and twisting roads can be challenging, so use caution and respect traffic rules. Be prepared for tiny roads and hairpin bends, and avoid speeding. It's also crucial to wear seat belts and use child safety seats when suitable.

Respect local customs and culture: Corsica has a unique culture and history, and it's crucial to respect the local customs and traditions. Dress modestly when visiting religious locations, and avoid insulting gestures or acts. Learn some simple French or Corsican phrases to converse with the people and show respect for their language. It's also crucial to be careful of the environment and conduct responsible tourism by not littering and respecting wildlife and nature.

Be cautious in distant regions: Corsica has several remote and secluded areas that may not have easy access to emergency services. If you plan to explore these locations, take extra precautions. Inform someone about your goals and expected time of return, carry a first-aid kit, and be prepared for limited phone reception. It's also advisable to examine weather conditions and local rules before traveling to isolated places.

By following these safety guidelines, you may assure a safe and pleasurable trip to Corsica. Remember to be mindful of the weather, take precautions in the water, be aware of hiking risks, protect your stuff, drive safely, respect local customs, and be cautious in remote locations. Prioritizing safety will help you make the most of your stay and create lasting memories of this gorgeous island.

Festival and Events

One of the most engaging parts of Corsican culture is its festivals and events, which are strongly based on its history, mythology, and local customs. Let's go into a thorough description of the festivals and events in Corsica, which exhibit the island's unique cultural identity.

One of the most prominent celebrations in Corsica is the Festival of Saint John, popularly known as "Festa di San Ghjuvanni." Held on the 23rd and 24th of June, this celebration symbolizes the summer solstice and honors the patron saint of Corsica, Saint John the Baptist. The celebration is celebrated with tremendous zeal, and the streets come alive with processions, bonfires, music, and dancing. Locals and visitors alike gather to witness the spectacle, which includes traditional Corsican polyphonic singing, known as "Cantu in paghjella," and folk dances performed in traditional costumes. The highlight of the festival is the lighting of bonfires, symbolizing the triumph of light over darkness, and the residents jumping over the flames for good luck.

Corsica is also recognized for its colorful music events. One of the most recognized is the Calvi Jazz Festival, held in the lovely village of Calvi in June or July. This festival attracts jazz aficionados from all over the world and involves concerts by local and worldwide jazz artists, as well as workshops and masterclasses for aspiring musicians. The festival takes place in numerous locales, including old churches, town centers, and outdoor venues, adding to its particular character.

Another prominent festival in Corsica is the Chestnut Festival, known as "A Festa di a Castagna." Held in November in the town of Bocognano, this festival pays honor to the chestnut, a key element in Corsican cuisine. The celebration contains traditional Corsican music, dances, and sports, and of course, an abundance of chestnut-based delicacies, such as roasted chestnuts, chestnut flour pancakes, and chestnut cake. It's a true celebration of Corsican culinary and agricultural heritage.

Corsica also holds various religious and cultural events throughout the year. One such event is the Procession of the Catenacciu, which takes place in the town of Sartene on Good Friday. This solemn procession comprises a penitent clad in a scarlet hooded gown, carrying a hefty wooden cross, and reenacts the crucifixion of Jesus Christ. The procession is a powerful exhibition of Corsican Catholic traditions and attracts visitors who want to witness this unique and solemn rite.

Corsica also conducts modern events that cater to varied interests. For example, the Corsica Raid Adventure is an exciting multi-sport race that takes place in several locations across the island, involving mountain biking, kayaking, trail running, and canyoning. This event attracts adventure enthusiasts from around the world and offers a unique chance to discover Corsica's breathtaking landscapes and challenging terrain.

In conclusion, Corsica's festivals and events are a vibrant expression of its rich cultural past and provide tourists with a unique opportunity to enjoy the island's customs, music, dance, food, and natural beauty. From religious processions to modern sports events, Corsica provides a broad choice of festivities that cater to different interests and create a completely immersing experience for travelers. Whether you're a music lover, a history buff, a foodie, or an adventure seeker, Corsica's festivals and events have something to offer for everyone. So, if you're planning a trip to Corsica, make sure to check the local schedule and immerse yourself in the colorful culture and festivities of this lovely Mediterranean island.

Printed in Great Britain
by Amazon